VERSES

FROM FEN AND FELL

VERSES

FROM FEN AND FELL

BY

THOMAS THORNELY

OF THE INNER TEMPLE, BARRISTER-AT-LAW
FORMERLY FELLOW OF TRINITY HALL, CAMBRIDGE

SECOND EDITION

(REVISED AND ENLARGED)

CAMBRIDGE
AT THE UNIVERSITY PRESS
1920

CAMBRIDGE UNIVERSITY PRESS
Cambridge, New York, Melbourne, Madrid, Cape Town,
Singapore, São Paulo, Delhi, Mexico City

Cambridge University Press
The Edinburgh Building, Cambridge CB2 8RU, UK

Published in the United States of America by Cambridge University Press, New York

www.cambridge.org
Information on this title: www.cambridge.org/9781107624054

© Cambridge University Press 1920

First edition 1919
Second (revised and enlarged) edition 1920
First published 1920
First paperback edition 2013

A catalogue record for this publication is available from the British Library

ISBN 978-1-107-62405-4 Paperback

TO MY SONS

R. R. T., D.S.C.
J. E. B. T., O.B.E. } R.A.F.

PREFACE TO FIRST EDITION

AMONG the many curious instincts which disturb and not infrequently discredit human nature, there is none which is more difficult to account for— since its 'survival value' must be of the slightest— than the mysterious impulse which leads so many of us, 'in an uncertain hour,' to break out into verse, and which persuades us so easily that crude thoughts and flippant fancies may be made presentable and even pleasing, if only they are tricked out with rhyme and metre.

Though the exact place of this obscure instinct in the general scale has not yet been determined by psychologists, we shall probably be safe in saying that it occupies a respectable position midway between those high instincts before which our guilty nature trembles and those which we have in common with the brutes, and the fact that reason has little or nothing to do with the matter will be felt to be less of a discredit at the present than at any previous time.

Being liable, like everything else that is worth having, to excess and abuse, it is the plain duty of everyone who feels it stirring within him to consider carefully how far it will be well for him to hold it in check, and to what extent it may be permitted free scope and exercise. There is danger in both directions, since a too severe repression may provoke an unwholesome eruption through some other vent, while a full indulgence can scarcely fail to cause annoyance to friends and acquaintances, who cannot always avail themselves of the remedy which the general public know so well how to use.

In my own case I have resorted to a compromise, giving timely utterance when the inward pressure has been severe and relief imperative, while, at the same time, showing consideration for others by allowing the results to remain hidden away in drawers and note-books.

An occasional peep or peer has been permitted to a few friends, on whose indulgence and discretion I have felt I could rely, and, if the stern resolution, on which I had rather plumed myself, has now broken down, I must invite them to take upon their own shoulders some portion of the responsibility and blame, since it is due to their friendly urgency that these callow owlets which I offer to Athens have been dragged from their snug obscurity and are now blinking and shivering in the light of day.

With respect to the form or mould into which I have cast my verse, it may possibly be noted with surprise that, though I have tried various measures, I have made no attempt at 'Vers libre,' which holds out so many attractions to the adventurous, and in which the poetic fancy of the day seems to find itself especially at home.

I am aware of course that some graceful, as well as many daring and surprising feats have been recently performed upon this particular spur of Parnassus, and I have often reproached myself for being unable to do more than sit and gasp at them in admiring wonder, but these treacherous peaks and precipices are no place for stiff joints and rheumatic brains and are better left to the happy audacity which vanishes with youth. If my thin piping is to be heard at all, it must be along the beaten and familiar tracks and under the restraining influence of rhyme and the old metrical conventions, however readily I may admit the superiority of those who feel that they can dispense with these aids and embellishments.

It will easily be seen, both from their subject-matter and from chance allusions, that several of the following verses were written long ago. Others are of yesterday and, though all alike are of the flimsiest texture and the lightest possible calibre, there are some among them on which the sobering influence of the times has set its mark, and which may be regarded as rude attempts to give expression to real feeling.

The various pieces follow one another with little or no attempt at order, and I must leave it to my readers to discover for themselves the golden thread of thought which binds them together. I may conclude by saying that I shall esteem them more fortunate than myself if they are able to find it.

T. T.

Merton Hall,
  Cambridge, 1919.

PREFACE TO SECOND EDITION

THE call for a new edition of these trivialities gives me a welcome opportunity of returning thanks to many kindly critics, who have not only refrained from trampling on my little patch of late-blossoming flowers, but have even affected to find fragrance here and there, and allowed themselves an occasional smile at my little pleasantries, when I had only too much reason to anticipate a disdainful sniff.

I should be better pleased, and feel that I was making a better return for this leniency, if I had been able to give an upward heave to the quality of my verse, instead of merely doubling its quantity, but the alternatives were not equally open to me and I fear the uplifting has not been great. To choose the lower course, while conscious that a better and higher exists, is often more of a necessity than a sin, though Ovid and the moralists (a rare conjunction!) seem to have had doubts about the point.

Even in so comparatively simple a matter as the correction of a faulty rhyme or the tuning of a jarring note, I have not always been able to act upon suggestion and remove the cause of offence, and must expect therefore to be set down as incorrigible and impenitent. Thus—though 'Kaiser' and 'Guyser' have severed their unseemly connection, and 'Torquemada' no longer adds a prosodic shudder to those which his name legitimately provokes, by rhyming himself with 'harder,' I have been obliged to abandon the attempt (after much vain poring over dictionaries) to find a better rhyme for 'Noah' than 'yore' and yet cannot bring myself to part company altogether with so engaging a figure as that of the great navigator and zoologist.

I admit the outrage and deplore the necessity for it, and can only plead in excuse that these Hebrew or Babylonian names are awkward and intractable things and that I am not the first rhymester to be brought into trouble by them.

If the Patriarch had been considerate enough to spell his name like the scene of the great naval mutiny (and who shall say with confidence that he did not do so?) all would have been well with me and a deadly shaft of criticism turned aside.

Another indulgent critic has tempered his praise by hinting that my notes are of yesterday.

This is quite true, but it could scarcely have been otherwise with me, and I have never indulged any arrogant hope of being classed with those on whom the spirit of a new age is deemed to have descended, and who are opening out on all sides fresh avenues of thought and expression.

It is enough for me if here and there a few are still to be found, for whom the old metrical forms and measures retain a lingering relish, and who are even able to take a sort of subdued pleasure in feeble and distant echoes of them.

For the rest—I have lopped and pruned with no sparing hand, in the hope of removing the more obvious blemishes, and have rooted out whole pieces when mere topiary work seemed insufficient and a more drastic method of gardening required.

Finding the exercise healthy and to my liking, I should probably have done more in this way if an authoritative voice had not called upon me peremptorily to desist, and told me to let bygones be bygones.

T. T.

Merton Hall,
  Cambridge, 1920.

CONTENTS

TWO WAYS OF LOOKING AT IT

Some say, and saying lightly laugh,
   'It were a fitter thing
If age would write it's epitaph,
   And leave the young to sing.

'Tis not on seamed and withered brow
   Castalian dews descend;
He who has held his peace till now
   Should hold it to the end.'

Some, kindlier, answer 'View it thus—
   To indulge a dotard's whim
Can do no serious harm to us,
   And may do good to him.

Then flap, O venerable bird!
   That worn dishevelled wing,
Let thy thin quavering notes be heard,
   Thy twilight twittering.'

CHAOS REDIVIVUS

A ray of hope has shivered through the gloom,
   Where, for long ordered ages, Chaos lies,
Blasts of Earth's fury rend his massy tomb,
   And faintly to his ears her frenzied cries
Come as awakening music, bidding him arise.

Dim memories stir of days when man to man
   Was wolf to wolf, and law within the pack
Was but the rule that he may take who can,
   When each exulted in his brother's lack;
Ah! blissful days, he sighs, could I but call them back!

T.   I   I

Now are they here, and, from the encumbering weight
   Of morals, manners, faiths and fashions, free,
Old Chaos rises, dons his robes of state,
   And sniffs reviving airs of anarchy.
If this should last, he cries, how happy we shall be!

The lights die down, his waning power oppressed
   In days far gone, love, reverence, brotherhood;
Loosed are the bonds of mutual interest,
   Earth reels and nothing stands where once it stood;
He looks enraptured round and softly murmurs—Good!

THE MALE MANTIS TO HIS MATE

(From facts supplied by M. Fabre)

Though to thine ardours I respond,
Full well I know my fate will be,
Through the dark hours to find thee fond,
Then make a morning meal for thee.

But, from some immemorial past,
Imperious promptings point the way
To love and death. Break then thy fast,
On me, at breaking of the day.

My love all other love excels,
Thine am I still when life has ceased;
For me alone the bridal bells
Ring in the bridegroom's funeral feast.

I know that instinct cannot err,
And love must lead through joy to gloom,
Then come, my executioner,
My loving wife and living tomb!

Possessing, I shall be possessed,
And indistinguishably thine.
Thou, my weird wife, art doubly blest,
With me to love, on me to dine!

'THE OLD WEST RIVER'

LARKS are singing round the Old West River,
  Coot are calling from the reeds below,
Golden shafts of morning break and shiver,
  Where the swallows, dipping, darting, come and go.

Scarce the name of what thou wast is left thee—
  Ouse is borne in shackles to the sea;
They that of thy store and strength bereft thee
  Left thee nothing but thy liberty.

Trickling runlets weep thy degradation,
  And in tears their tiny tribute pay,
Healing drops that kept thee from stagnation,
  When thy native springs were borne away.

Emblem art thou of a form forsaken
  By its quickening soul, a creed outworn;
Husk thou art, from which the seed is shaken;
  Truth, from all its living context torn.

All that made thee great has gone for ever;
  None shall lead thine exiled waters home;
Yet some there are that love the Old West River,
  And share its peace, when by its bank they roam

QUERIES

WERE every wrong redressed,
Right everywhere prevailing,
Would Virtue unresisted rest,
Its fount of action failing?
No! Heaven would plan another quest,
Spread other seas for sailing.

Were every wish fulfilled,
That sets us now a sighing,
Would pleasure's clanking wheels be stilled,
The stream that turns them drying?
No! Other wants would soon be willed,
New wheels be set a flying.

If knowledge all were known,
And error all transcended,
Would mind sit idle on its throne,
Its work and mission ended?
No! truth would other aspects own,
With other error blended.

Man lives but as he strives,
In death alone is resting;
'Tis but the mounting soul survives,
Fresh heights for ever breasting;
Heaven's but a home for strenuous lives,
That stood Earth's hour of testing.

THE ATOM

"We do not in the least know how to harness the energy locked up in the atoms of matter. If it could be liberated at will, we should experience a violence beside which the suddenness of high explosive is gentle and leisurely."

Sir O. LODGE.

WAKE not the imprisoned power that sleeps,
Unknown, or dimly guessed, in thee!
Thine awful secret Nature keeps,
And pales, when stealthy science creeps
Towards that beleaguered mystery.

Well may she start and desperate strain,
To thrust the bold besiegers back;
If they that citadel should gain,
What grisly shapes of death and pain
May rise and follow in their track!

The power that warring atoms yield,
Man has to guiltiest purpose turned.
Too soon the wonder was revealed,
Earth flames in one red battle-field;
Could but that lesson be unlearned!

Thy last dread secret, Nature! keep;
Add not to man's tumultuous woes;
Till war and hate are laid to sleep,
Keep those grim forces buried deep,
That in thine atoms still repose.

THE AMOEBA

Amoeba! O mother of all that lives,
And of life that is yet to be;
First of the forms to which Nature gives,
Her promise and potency;
Far and high have thy children climbed, they are climbing
still;
Why dost thou linger, Amoeba, alone at the foot of the hill?

They have peopled the earth, the sea and the air,
They run, they swim and they fly;
Many and strange are the forms they wear,
As they mingle and multiply.
Armed are they all and equipped for the fight thou dost not
begin,
And the fleeter of foot, the fiercer of fang and the craftier win.

Amoeba! abidest thou still in thy tent,
Like Achilles or Israel?
Why cling to thy simple environment,
Thy life in a single cell?
Is it modesty, cowardice, sloth, withholds thee from enter-
prise?
Thou canst do what thy children have done and are doing,
Awake and arise!

Sayest thou—many have tried and failed,
Why should we care to try?
Right has perished and wrong prevailed,
In a world that is wrought awry.
Better to brood in the depths, sayest thou, than to scale the
height,
Only to falter and fail, or sink to the shame of the parasite.

6

What are the 'fitter,' but they that grow
A deadlier tooth or claw?
If they get them knowledge, 'tis but to know
That to struggle is Nature's law.
Few are the forms of life that succeed, and what is success?
A wider field for a deadlier fight, a more resolute ruthlessness.

Progress is mockery, growth disease,
There are men who have known it well,
They have lived in a tub, like Diogenes,
Or a hermit's single cell.
Wise were they, spurning the life they had led and the race
       they had run,
But wiser and happier we, who foreseeing have never begun.

But bethink thee, Amoeba, of those who win
To the highest, and claim as the prize
The Will, the Soul that can trample sin,
And the Love that sanctifies!
Long and rough is the road, but call not the process vain,
Which leads, from the mindless deeps, to such glories, be-
       think thee again.

Tell me of this, when the goal is in sight,
When man is a lover of men,
In the dust and din of a world-wide fight,
I laugh, but may listen then.
While the lordliest cherish the hate in their heart, and glory
       in strife,
The lowliest well may live as at first, at the foot of the ladder
       of life.

7

THE LADYBIRD AND THE DANDELION

O LADYBIRD! that, with forlorn endeavour,
Searchest the wild-flower for its sealèd wine,
The golden lure may urge thee on for ever,
But not one drop, one sip, shall e'er be thine!

Why was the unavailing impulse given?
Have mocking Powers ordained thee to the quest?
Art thou by aimless eyeless forces driven,
Or lives there meaning in thy deep unrest?

Dost thou, in seeking one thing, find another?
As Saul, in search of asses, found a throne,
As one, who gives his all to aid his brother,
Finds that the richer gain has been his own.

Though man's high longings be denied fruition,
His footsteps never reach the yearned-for goal,
The broken fragments of a baulked ambition
May prove a ladder for the ascending soul.

His cherished vision of a gem-built Zion
Has shaped for man a brighter world below;
Thy unslaked thirst in the gold Dandelion
May bring thee bliss which else thou could'st not know.

If this my hope for thee be but illusion,
And Science knows no reconciling word,
Deep in thine inner essence sits confusion;
Thou hast a problem set, O Ladybird!

THE AFFLATUS

THERE are certain times and seasons when the verse-evolving
    brain
Finds, for no apparent reasons, that invention is in vain,
When the threads of thought lie broken round the shuttle
    and the wheel,
And the merry bells of fancy sound like muffled funeral peal;
When the mind looks out on all about with dull incurious
    eyes,
And over all there hangs a pall that stifles enterprise.

You invoke the Muse for vision, and she tells you to your face,
With a smile of sweet derision, that your style is commonplace;
You may seek Pierian fountain, but the faithless stream is
    dry,
And the peaked Parnassian mountain seems unconscionably
    high;
If you court the aid of Pegasus, you will find him out at grass,
And he snorts you back his answer 'Do you take me for an
    ass?'

E'en heavenly Powers have known these hours, the pipe of
    Pan is still,
The Graces yawn within their bowers, the Muses on their hill;
Apollo, with his bow unbent, lays golden harp aside,
And Orpheus ceases to lament his twice abandoned bride;
Oread and Dryad, nymph and faun their sprightly dance
    forego,
The Triton drops his wearied horn and dives to depths
    below,
And languid all Olympus lies, aloof from thought or care,
Looking with unresponsive eyes on lips that move in prayer.

There are times, in short, for soaring thought, and times for
    folded wing,
When fancy plods and Nature nods and nothing cares to sing;
No billow's roar offends the shore, no tempest frets the deep,
And e'en the willow bending o'er his brook forgets to weep;
Each songster to his thicket flies, the bees have ceased to
    hum,
'Tis not the wise who poetise, when these dead hours have
    come.
If thought should twinge you then, as gout will tingle in the
    toes,
'Tis best no doubt to work it out, but—let it be in prose.

A WILTING FLOWER

Out of what bitter soil, sad flower,
    From what infected air,
Came that which, in thine opening hour,
    Makes frustrate all my care?

I set thee midst thy smiling peers,
    And bade thee bloom as they,
When each its blushing crest uprears
    To greet adoring day.

Full share hadst thou of sunny showers,
    And yet the ranging bee,
That wantons with thy sister flowers,
    Turns, as in scorn, from thee.

Soft on thee fell the morning dew,
  As soft eve's humid breath,
Yet, ere the stars their watch renew,
  Thy petals droop in death.

So, from a common home of love,
  Nurtured with equal care,
Some hearts will mirror heaven above,
  Some sink—we know not where.

THE IGUANODON

(A down-hearted dinosaur)

OR, PATHOS IN THE PRIME

WHEN Life, aglow with primal glee,
Pranked in weird shapes that now are gone,
And Nature wantoned wild and free,
It was my curious fate to be
A thing that now you seldom see—
    An Iguanodon.

Creative power, since kindlier grown,
To me, alas! was all unkind.
It heaped upon me flesh and bone,
Till every limb had monstrous grown,
As if it cared for bulk alone,
    But stinted me in mind.

If I could live my life again,
I should with my creator plead—
E'en at the price of sin and pain—
For just an added ounce of brain;
A life so utterly inane
    Is not a life to lead.

For ever loitering in the slime,
Or browsing on preposterous trees,
I felt the weary weight of time:
In that debilitating clime,
My whole existence seemed a crime
    And void of power to please.

I had no aspirations high,
No yearnings for the upper air,
No impulse came to scale the sky,
And life's mysterious source defy,
No frenzied wish to dare or die,
    No wrestlings with despair.

But, waddling on the unstable earth,
Or paddling in the tepid sea,
Musing alone, in joyless mirth,
I asked myself what life was worth,
And what could justify the birth,
    Of fatuous things like me.

Could I but think the powers I lack
Lay hid, to be in time revealed,
Feel friendly pressure at my back—
But no! I know the appointed track
Led but to Nature's cul de sac,
    And that my fate was sealed.

I was no herald of the dawn,
Forerunner of a race to be,—
A race, whose proud exalted horn
Might yet avenge an age's scorn,
By fiery domination born
    In far futurity—

No hopes of empire shook my rest,
Or tinged my pale innocuous dreams;
Shrinking from Nature's sterner test,
Between the oppressor and the oppressed,
I stood as one who counts it blest
    To shudder at extremes.

No spark from passion's smouldering fire
Glowed ever in my listless eyes,
Stirred my sick soul to generous ire,
Or drew me from the deadening mire;
I never felt the least desire
    For any enterprise.

So, numbed by sloth and sunk in shame,
I yawned my useless life away—
A life without a single aim,
A life intolerably tame—
When death and dissolution came,
They did but call me from a game
    I had no mind to play[1].

Yet you, to whom a generous share
Of brains, so grudged to me, has gone,
Press round my bones to peep and stare,
As though a genius rested there,
And guard with ceremonious care
    An Iguanodon!

[1] The poor afflicted monster has allowed his honest indignation to carry him a line too far, but I had not the heart to pull him up. (T. T.)

13

TO CERTAIN PHILOSOPHERS

EVIL, ye say, is goodness read awry,
And folly wisdom in a wayward mood;
In clear-eyed vision contradictories die,
And difference melts into similitude.

Choose but, ye say, some loftier coign of view,
And mark how misery dissolves in bliss,
Vice turns herself to virtue, false to true,
Fused in some reconciling synthesis.

Judge not, nor sift the sinners from the saints,
Call not Aurelius good or Borgia bad:
In the full glare of truth, distinction faints,
And Gawain ranks with spotless Galahad.

Take a proud nation's blazoned roll of fame,
And blot, with undiscriminating pen,
Each word of praise, each shadowy hint of shame,
And write—'These were as are all other men.'

Links are we all of one eternal chain,
Dragged, why we know not, up life's steep ascent;
Sin is illusion and remorse is vain;
To prate of freedom is but babblement.

Wrong is, so say ye, but the temporal name
Men give to aspects of eternal right.—
We hear and answer, 'End the wordy game,
And crown your creed by adding—Black is White!'

FEN AND FELL

TIME was I thought the mountain's airy brow,
Sea-scented dunes, and lonely moorland glens,
Held all Earth's beauty I could love, but now
I seek and find it round me in the Fens.

I love to gaze where lines of willowed grey
The plain's green glory temper and subdue,
While, on the dim horizon far away,
Earth's grey and green melt into Heaven's own blue.

Here gleam and drowse fair streams that never yet
Have murmured out the song that in them sleeps;
E'en when their bordering osiers toss and fret,
In winter storm, their soul its silence keeps.

Such streams are they as through Elysium glide,
Their banks by undying blossoms overhung,
Or where Boeotian marsh-lands far and wide
Lie dreaming of the songs the Graces sung.

Where yon far fane towers high o'er swamp and sward,
The raven-beaked barge of Knut has stayed its oar,
At vesper song; here leaguered Hereward
Flamed back defiance to the Conqueror.

And, where the sun dips down till, like a dome,
It rests upon the horizon, reddening all
The long low levels, Cromwell left his home
And Ouse-bound meadows, at his country's call.

These homeward-faring rooks shall find their rest,
Where Cambridge in her desolation lies,
Mourning the sons she nourished at her breast;
Her life was theirs; with them she daily dies.

Where stealthy mists, up-gathering from the plain,
Meet and conspire to weave the shroud of day,
Still creeps the tide that bore the treacherous Dane,
His burning heart athirst for spoil and prey.

Like some vast heave of ocean's swelling blue,
Yon eastern uplands rise and mark the scene
Where Rome's impetuous eagles vengeful flew,
And screamed around the Iceni's hapless queen.

Larks scatter round Heaven's largesse from on high,
In golden song, and, when they cease to sing,
Earth answers with the peewit's plaintive cry,
As low she brushes with deceitful wing,

With flute of sedge-screened fowl, the quavering sound
Of drumming snipe, or honk of watchful hern;
Each day, or heard or seen, fresh joy is found,
Some lesson taught I am new-skilled to learn.

Yet tax me not with an inconstant love,
If I have ceased to pine that never here,
When the clouds break, I look on peaks above,
Or see below a rock-encircled mere.

Though to my heart new scenes their message send,
They mingle there with joys of long ago;
Life's swollen river, broadening to its end,
More varied beauty mirrors than youth could know.

CAT AND DOG

(*A Difference of Temperament*)

O SLIGHTED useless pains! What profit lies
In pouring praise on dull regardless ears?
I dubbed thee beautiful, acclaimed thee wise,
And called the world to witness that thine eyes
Outshone in lustre all the starry spheres.
      That cold inscrutable heart I could not stir,
      Nor win so much as one approving purr!

Were but the half of what I squandered spent
In adulation on thine enemy,
It had upreared such mountains of content,
Unsealed such founts of slobbering sentiment,
As had turned love to flat idolatry.
      Thy finer taste counts such ebullience crude,
      And deems emotion but disquietude!

ABDICATION

TAKE my last greeting, ye compacted Powers!
That, for some hidden purpose, met in me,
Fashioning the frame o'er which, in conscious hours,
I exercise an unsought sovereignty.

Cell upon cell the mystic fabric rose,
The woven tissues shaped themselves to man,
A measured music shook me from repose,
As through my heart life's quickening current ran.

No will of mine it was that brought me here;
I woke to find myself upon a throne;
My kingdom broadened round me year by year,
Till I could call an ordered world my own.

Obedient slaves, that ne'er from duty swerved,
Compassed me round and fed my lightest whim,
Not Heaven itself is more obsequious served
By angel guards and white-robed seraphim.

They found for me a fit environment,
Drew from it all that might my needs supply;
Did danger threaten, swift the warning went,
Unseen battalions bade the intruder fly.

If, swollen with thoughtless pride, I mocked at fear,
Squandered my powers, or rode with loosened rein,
A trusty counsellor whispered in my ear
Hints of disorder, presages of pain.

So, year by year, I drew exulting breath,
Rejoicing in a well-established sway,
Till, at my court, the ambassador of Death
Threw down his challenge, ere he went his way.

Now slackening sinews tell of inward strife,
The legions mutter that the hour is nigh,
When revolution in the realm of life
Shall bid me lay the imperial sceptre by.

So be it! not by me was empire sought,
I freely render what ye freely gave;
Yet temper this your triumph by the thought—
'Tis you, not I, descend into the grave.

AGANELLA

"Some write that Aganella, a fair maid of Corcyra, was the inventor of it, for she presented the first ball that ever was made to Nausicaa, the daughter of King Alcinous, and taught her how to use it."

(Burton's *Anatomy of Melancholy*.)

WHAT were life without its leisure?
What were leisure without play?
Play without a ball were pleasure
With half its sweetness sucked away.

Aganella of Corcyra!
Hadst thou what is rightly thine,
Every youth were an admirer,
Every maid would deck thy shrine.

Thou hadst been acclaimed by Clio;
Blazoned on her scroll of worth
Thy name, like gadfly-goaded Io,
Had wandered over all the earth.

Poets, who have all ignored thee,
With hearts that burned and eyes that shone,
Had in rapturous phrase adored thee,
From Pindus and from Helicon.

Only Burton's pedant pages
Lift from thee oblivion's pall;
Sport, he argues, spleen assuages,
Citing Aganella's ball.

She the first ball wrought and rounded,
In her Ionian isle afar;
Tossed it, tested, found it bounded,
And sent it to Nausicaa.

Homer sings how, linen-laden,
From her kingly father's hall,
The wrecked Ulysses met the maiden,
And watched her as she tossed the ball.

But the blind bard says no word of
The god-like girl from whom it came,
Aganella, hardly heard of,
Be it ours to sing thy fame!

What though history doubtful eyes thee!
Let us—scorning fact and date—
Strive to apotheosize thee,
And a kind of cult create.

Was thy parting soul transported,
In the grand old Grecian way,
To the Olympian courts and courted
By the lucent lords of day?

Hast thou played and danced and dallied,
Where the great gods sip their wine,
And, in regions dim and pallid,
Cheered the gloom of Proserpine?

Did thy ball, blest Aganella!
Draw favouring smile from many a god,
And e'en from the awful Cloud-Compeller
Win for thee one world-shaking nod?

Wast thou bidden by Apollo,
Bending from his amber car,
In his burning track to follow,
As a tributary star?

Art thou seen, when dawn is breaking,
Driving from an eternal 'tee,'
And an awesome 'foursome' making
With Orion's flaming three?

Didst thou challenge bright Aurora—
Old Tithonus whimpering by—
To a 'set,' to triumph o'er her
And send her blushing down the sky?

Or, to amuse a listless Heaven,
Hast thou, on Elysian lawn,
Captained an elect eleven
Of nymph and dryad, sylph and faun?

Haply gorgon, satyr or centaur,
While the applauding thunder rolls,
Takes the ball from its inventor
And 'twisters' diabolic bowls.

Do thine astral muscles harden,
Beneath the golden-fruited trees
Of the dragon-guarded garden,
Sporting with the Hesperides?

In thy darker mood thou strayest
From thy bright ambrosial bliss,
And a sombre 'single' playest
In the dusky courts of Dis.

On the meads of Asphodel a
Pale but interested shade
Mows the links where Aganella
With the disembodied played,

With the scythe of Saturn mowing;
Charon and a crew of souls
Bunkers build while, panting, blowing,
Sisyphus the surface rolls.

All the Stygian air is thrilling
With rumours of the 'next event,'
Gibbering ceases, bat-like shrilling
Turns to babblings of content.

Even in Hell's unhealthiest section,
Where toil and pain unpitied pant,
Some there are have caught the infection,
And made them balls of adamant.

Once from sulphurous throats there broke a
Cheer, when some Tartarean ghost
Aganella's ball did croquet,
As it neared the winning-post.

And the Fire-King, shrouded, sable,
With rumblings earth and heaven appal,
Rolls out a storm-built billiard-table,
With thunderbolt for billiard-ball.

May we think thy bright ball bounces,
When some meteoric star
On the earth from ether pounces,
Like Perseus on Andromeda?

Some may court the Sister Graces,
Some invoke the Muses nine,
Doubtless all had comely faces
And gifts—but what are theirs to thine?

Thou hast glory from the glorious,
Soberer homage from the slow,
Thou art where the fun's uproarious,
Thou art where the golfers go.

Aganella! gracious golden
Memories float around us all,
Who have been to thee beholden
For that priceless boon—the ball.

'OUGHT' AND 'IS'

PROUD Science, from her conquering car,
    Surveys her realm from error won;
'To me,' she cries, 'all gates unbar,
    My laws shall unresisted run,
Though man may bend reluctant knee,
And idly prate of liberty.'

Twixt 'ought' and 'is' a gulf profound
    Confronts her, as she seeks to prove
Man's will in causal chains is bound,
    And moves but in its fated groove;
This unbridged chasm wrecks all her plan
Of showing nature one with man.

Vainly the void she seeks to fill
    With ponderous verbiage; still the abyss
Yawns; vainly dialectic skill
    Thrusts out wide arms of synthesis.
No bridge may span that gulf of thought,
Still is is is and ought is ought!

THE ESK AND MUNCASTER

There is Esk that meets the Solway sand,
And Esk by northern sea,
But the Esk of rocky Cumberland
Is the fairest of the three;
  I watch its grey-green waters pass
  From Muncaster to Ravenglass.

Its springs are where yon cloud is seen,
'Neath England's loftiest crest[1],
Mid rocks that house the peregrine
And guard the raven's nest,
  Beyond that ridge of fading blue
  Where once the Roman eagles flew[2].

Esk looked on many a borderer's fray,
Heard many a clash of spear,
And when the White Rose won the day,
The Red Rose harboured here,
  In peel that mourns its glory gone
  With the last lordly Pennington.

The pledge of England's hapless king
Now lies dishonoured there,
Its power no more avails to bring
The rashly-promised heir[3],
  Alas that seer and saint should err!
  The Stranger rules in Muncaster.

[1] Sca-Fell Pike.   [2] Hardknot Camp.
[3] Henry VI gave to Sir John Pennington an enamelled glass chalice known as the 'Luck of Muncaster' with the assurance that, so long as it remained unbroken, a male heir should never be wanting to the Penningtons of Muncaster.
Lord Muncaster died recently without an heir.

'I AM A PART OF ALL THAT I HAVE MET'

(TENNYSON)

IF men are made by all they meet,
As sages say and poet sings,
I must be packed from head to feet
With other people's thoughts and things;
Each casual touch contagion brings
Of good or bad, of sour or sweet,
Of devil's horns or angel's wings.
    I am in short, a curious blend
    Of pilfered parts of foe and friend.

I was endowed, ere I was born,
With dubious gifts of various kind,
With traits and tricks that, frayed and worn,
Ancestral owners left behind—
All in a hopeless tangle twined—
Nor from its context can be torn
The thing I fondly call my mind.
    What am I then supposed to be?
    How much of what is mine is me?

Philosophy cold comfort gives—
'Of one all-comprehending whole
A facet, phase, or aspect lives,
And plays an evanescent rôle—
Like bubble in a boiling bowl—
Though some with proud prerogatives
Invest it, as the seat of soul;
    That phase of thought, that point of view,
    If you are anything—is you!'

25

RAVENGLASS

ANCHOR never more may drop below thee,
Silting sands have barred thy seaward way,
Few that in thy degradation know thee,
Guess the glory of thy former day.

Rome has sought thee, Danes have camped around thee,
Dynasties and empires rise and pass,
Since the first Phoenician trader found thee,
Mid thy lone sea-ridges, Ravenglass!

Gathering-ground of old and vanished races,
Thou hast watched the legions come from far,
Seen the light of victory flush their faces,
Heard them sing or sigh for Capua.

Thou hast played thy part in England's story,
Sent thy sons to many a distant fray,
Won thy meed of mingled grief and glory,
When they died for England far away.

Guard, O guard thine ancient isolation,
Veil thyself from undiscerning eye,
Covet not the rabble's admiration,
Bid the boisterous tripper bustle by.

Grudge him not his hour of noisy pleasure,
Wince not if a passing gibe he throw;
Deep within thee lies thy hidden treasure,
In the buried worth of long ago.

Not to garish youth comes pleasure only;
O'er thine age a tempered joy may steal;
Seek the consolation of the lonely;
Cherish eye to see and heart to feel.

Three fair rivers here their waters mingle,
Ere they win a laughing welcome from the deep;
Let their voices, as they ripple o'er thy shingle,
Whisper comfort to thee in thy sleep.

Myriad sea-fowl float and glance above thee,
From their sanctuary by the sea,
Unmolested there they live and love thee,
Thy decay is their security.

Life has need of lonely silent spaces,
Where the burdened soul may cast its care,
Ponder on the past and meet the embraces
Of a sea-born, hope-illumined air.

Still, as stand the mountains round about thee,
Stand and meet the future, Ravenglass!
Though a busy world ignore or flout thee,
As thine own, so shall its glory pass.

TO THE FAINT-HEARTED

(If there are any such) (1915)

GET ye pipes of scrannel straw;
Ease your sick heart of its complaining;
Bring ye sprays of Hellebore,
Gathered when the moon is waning;
    Pipe away your fear and folly,
    Purge your soul of melancholy!

27

Unlace the buskin, school your feet
To tread some less lugubrious measure;
Bid every sickly fancy fleet,
Each sighing breath ye fondly treasure.
    Comb out the ashes from your hair,
    Nor longer woe's black wimple wear.

Your girdle break of threaded tears—
Each drop distilled from grief unspoken—
Put off your robe of woven fears,
The emblem of a spirit broken.
    Pack your sad fripperies in a pall,
    Heave one last sigh—then bury all!

Drain the cup of trembling dry,
And fill it with a generous potion,
To flash some lightning to your eye,
And set your curdling blood in motion.
    Through flaccid veins let wild-fire pass,
    Burning your doubts like withered grass.

Not by fainting hearts was built
The realm our sons have died defending;
And not for such their blood is spilt,
The vigour spent, which they are spending.
    They ask of us, who hold them dear,
    One stern resolve—No faltering here!

HOPE AND PATIENCE

STRETCH, wider stretch thine arms, immortal Hope!
Eternal Patience, let us learn of thee,
With Earth's immeasurable woes to cope,
Our hearts high held above despondency.

Let not the harvest of these angry years
Rot in our fields, our travail all be vain,
But let the seed, in sorrow sown and tears,
Bring forth its increase, turning loss to gain.

Though through our heart deep drives War's bitter share,
Bid us remember years of drought and blight,
Call to our minds what weeds were harbouring there,
What god-like potencies denied the light.

As heaven, for many an age, with radiance bright
Of unsuspected stars was thickly sown,
So youth's wild glory beacons from many a height
Unscaled before, to youth itself unknown.

Though Earth's best blood in countless streams has run,
And on her fields lain like the morning dew,
When plough and harrow and a kindlier sun
Have done their work, what harvests rise to view!

Grain such as in no earthly furrow grows,
From rust of sloth and blight of faction free,
And freshened by the breeze that ever blows
About the star-crowned head of Liberty.

THE DARDANELLES, 1915

IT is an autumn evening fair;
Far up among the lonely fells,
There beats upon the dreaming air
The faint familiar call to prayer,
The sound of distant village bells.

And all around the heather blooms,
Of peace each streamlet tinkling tells,
But over all a shadow glooms,
And ever in my ear there booms
The thunder of the Dardanelles.

Save where some too laborious bee
Brings murmurous hints of busy care,
All nature breathes tranquillity,
But to that vexed and sinuous sea,
My troubled thoughts perforce repair.

Where Greek and Trojan met of old,
For ever locked in deathless fray;
Where Hero met Leander bold,
And Jason brought his fleece of gold,
Embattled empires meet today.

Here, borne by Freedom's battle-breeze,
From many a famed and distant land,
From western isles and southern seas,
E'en from the far Antipodes,
The new crusaders mustering stand.

One common hope in life they share,
And in that hope they proudly die,
That never more may tyrant dare
To poison peace and taint the air,
Where Freedom's flag is wont to fly.

MY DAUGHTER'S DOG

DEAR is my daughter, dear her dog
(To her); they live with me,
And, for a time, we seemed to jog
Along harmoniously.
  Like triple star that flames on high,
  We shone, the daughter, dog and I.

Then I began to insinuate
(Ah! Would that it were true!)
That, in that dread triumvirate,
I bossed the other two.
  Perhaps, presuming on the thought,
  I showed a somewhat 'swelling port.'

I said the dog was Lepidus,
(A sorry dog was he,)
Myself the august Octavius,
My daughter Antony,
  And history, I made it plain,
  Might soon repeat itself again!

But now, if ever comes a tiff,
Betwixt my child and me,
We still may ask and argue if
We are not Antony.
  But facts have brought it home to us,
  That neither is Octavius.

Yet, though (to put it at the worst)
The dog has won the day,
And from the last become the first,
Beneath my breath, I say,
  'There's nothing in the Decalogue
  Bids me obey my daughter's dog.'

IN A GOTHIC CATHEDRAL

PEACE! think ye peace these towering piers express?
  Those clustering shafts, yon heavenward-soaring arch?
Alert they stand, the embodiment of stress,
Type of the soul's eternal sleeplessness,
  Each stone a warrior ever on the march.

Of strife they speak, unending eager strife,
  Taut sinews, throbbing veins and labouring breath,
Did but one pier relax its strenuous life,
O'er nave and aisle disruption would be rife,
  And through the breach would storm beleaguering death.

If rest ye seek, dull massive dreamless rest,
  Turn, eastward turn, those undiscerning eyes;
Far from the flaming fervours of the West,
Its fevered hopes, in tortured stone expressed,
  The pillared pomp of Egypt scrutinise.

Search the lone wastes, lay bare from desert dust
  The shattered remnants of Assyrian pride,
In mindless soulless strength these put their trust,
No straining arch found there its lateral thrust
  Countered by craft, by stubborn art defied.

If, viewing with equal scorn barbarian might
  And mystic rapture born of faith obscure,
Ye crave proportion, balance, breadth and light,
Let Doric fanes uplift for your delight
  Their fluted shafts and graven entablature.

There clear-eyed Reason donned her queenliest dress,
  Making dull matter glow with hidden mind,
Reflecting in each line life's loveliness,
Yet recked she nothing of the soul's distress,
  All is of earth, no hint of heaven we find.

'DOWN AMONG THE MARSHES'

THERE is peace among the mountains, I have known it long
    ago,
But the mountains ask for muscle that my limbs no longer
    show,
  So I bid adieu to climbing, since it may no better be,
  Thinking—down among the marshes lies the land for me.

Let others seek their pleasure on parade or on the pier,
I sincerely hope they find it, but my hope lies here,
  Where the willows bend above me and the cattle graze
    below,
  And the dusky wide-winged barges on the broad stream go.

I watch the noisy motors, as they thunder on their way
To the scenes where crowds are thronging and the bands for
    ever bray,
  Then I seek the open spaces, where the larks are on the
    wing,
  Where the coot are ever calling, and the marsh birds sing.

To the far-off dim horizon there is nothing to be seen
But silver threads of water set in grey blue green,
  Swallows flit and dart about me, and the stately herons pass,
  As I lie beside the lilies in the deep lush grass.

While, in distance faintly shining, like a lone ship on the main,
The grey cathedral city lifts her towers above the plain.
  Here is peace for all who ask it, here is joy for all who care
  For the kindly scents of homely earth, deep draughts of
    honest air;
Let others boast the beauty of the mountain and the sea,
But—down among the marshes lies the land for me.

THREE VOICES IN AMERICA

FIRST VOICE

Vox Clamantis (1915)

THE stars that on thy banner burn
Show faint and dim today,
Like tapers round the funeral urn
Of honour passed away;
    Their home is freedom's native air,
    They may not shine dishonoured there.

They led thee, when a tyrant's hand
Thy rising power repressed,
From bondage to a promised land,
By God's own bounty blessed.
    They were the heaven-born stars that shone
    On Lincoln, Lee and Washington.

By might of manhood, pride of race,
And hearts uplifted high,
Thy son's have won Earth's proudest place,
Thy stars have scaled the sky;
    They set the old world's captive free,
    And flamed in glory on the sea.

But now thy leaders sit aloof,
Thy stars look coldly down,
Though, 'neath the invader's lawless hoof,
Lies many a ruined town.
    From blackened hearth and shattered fane,
    Belgium has cried to thee in vain!

A tyrant's rage has set at nought
The bond thy hand had sealed.
His victims fight, as thou hast fought,
On freedom's fatal field.
    O, say not that thy heart is cold,
    And beats not as it beat of old!

Had but rebuking word of thine
Been flashed across the seas;
Did but thy stars indignant shine
On nameless infamies,
    The baffled tyrant's heart had quailed,
    And law, now mocked and spurned, prevailed.

Die down, ye lights, in glory lit,
Ye hopes so proudly cherished.
What place is yours, if Mammon sit
Where Right has ruled and perished?
    If black dishonour veil the skies,
    That saw the star-sown banner rise?

SECOND VOICE

Vox Pacifica (1915)

Let thy bewildered wailing cease!
These mourned-for stars of thine
High in the midmost heaven of peace,
With undimmed radiance shine.
    No red war-kindling orbs are they,
    Their march is on the Milky Way.

Still their predestined course they keep,
Though realms in ruin fall;
Serene they neither smile nor weep,
When anguished nations call,
But wait, in patient undismay,
The dawning of a soberer day.

Not theirs to guide a ravening horde,
O'er seas of blood and woe.
The Western World disdains the sword,
And sheathed it long ago.
Though Freedom, smitten to the core,
Shrieks for her aid, she fights no more.

She joins not in the proud acclaim,
When honour greatly dies;
She envies not the victor's fame,
Or the blood-purchased prize.
To her the Old World's tumults seem
Dim shapes of some distempered dream.

Not hers the guilt, if greed and hate
Set half the world aflame;
She cannot bid the storm abate,
Or war's wild passions tame.
With breaking hearts and tottering thrones,
The Old World for her sin atones.

But when, with shame and guilt oppressed,
Her deadly discords dead,
In penitential garments dressed,
With ashes on her head,
Europe shall quit her bed of pain,
And stagger to her feet again,

In faltering tones she then shall say,
'To me, alas! 'twas given
To tread the ungodly's darkened way
And scorn the path of Heaven.
Would that Columbia's choice were mine!'
Then shall our stars benignant shine.

Till then, unmoved by scorn or threat,
With eyes and conscience clear,
Howe'er a mad world rage and fret,
Our star-lit course we steer.
Though tongues may taunt and brows may bend,
We hold our purpose to the end.

THIRD VOICE

Vox Vera (1917)

Hushed was each voice,—a silence fell,
Till, gathering from afar,
More fiercely blazed, like fires of Hell,
The ever-widening war,
And Europe's unimagined woes
Thrilled through the West:—Columbia rose.

A storm of angered awed surprise
Across her spirit broke,
Her stars' wild glory filled her eyes,
As thus incensed she spoke,—
While tortured nations felt again
Hope tingle in each quivering vein:—

Think not, because our Powers delayed
To explore the fiery deep,
We looked in danger's face dismayed,
Or held our honour cheap.
    In counselling right, rebuking wrong,
    And hoping much, we lingered long.

On ancient wisdom were we reared,
Befitting Freedom's wards,
'Mix not'—had said a voice revered—
'With Europe's wrangling lords';
    And proud traditions, old and tried,
    We may not lightly thrust aside.

But we have seen a perjured band
Each law of God defy,
Seen outrage stalking through our land,
Our sons in ocean die;
    No more we bend before the blast,
    The cup is full, the die is cast!

From rusting sheath the sword we draw,
Which sheathless shall remain,
Till Right has conquered Might, and Law
Keeps guard o'er Greed and Gain.
    Our stars shine, till that hour shall come,
    In air that vibrates with the drum.

THE OWL

LET others seek, through storm and strife,
Their places in the sun;
For us the only hours of life
Are when the day is done.
    When eve is here, we softly flit,
    And whispered welcomes waft *to it*.

Some praise the all-blistering fount of day,
And joy in sultry noon;
It makes us wonder whether they
Have ever seen the moon.
    Ah! gracious queen, no lover true
    But learned beneath thy beams *to woo*.

O'er dusky woods we watch her rise,
And meadows drenched in dew;
From the mild radiance of her eyes,
Our eyes their strength renew.
    Though men, with dull laborious wit,
    Our day-dimmed eyes deride and *twit*.

Let dotards dream in bower and house,
What can they know or feel,
Who never chased the midnight mouse,
Or heard the leveret squeal?
    With joy and rapture thrilling through,
    We sound the hunter's wild *Halloo-oo*!

One race alone of human-kind
Has given the owl her due;
They first from man's neglected mind
Its grace and wisdom drew;
    And bade the owl in glory sit—
    Beside Athene's throne *to wit*.

Come, silent flitting as the bat,
Ere furry poachers prowl,
Let not the intruding, shameless cat
Boast that she ousts the owl.
    May many a deed of derring-do
    Be done tonight, *To-whit-to-whoo*!

RECONCILIATION

GOLDEN grass and rusting heather,
And the many-tinted fern,
Mix their fragrant breath together,
And together glow and burn.
    Life and death, in beauty blending
    All their former grace transcending.

Friend and foe together lying,
On the torn and trampled plain,
Turn to one another dying,
Soothing one another's pain.
    Life in love and duty ending;
    Gracious be their souls' ascending.

Though the War's afflicting thunder
Leave us withered as the grass,
Sins that tore our souls asunder,
With the passing storm may pass;
    Class with class no more contending,
    Fused in fire from Heaven descending.

ON PARTING WITH A PET RAVEN

ABANDONED bird! A freak of fancy led me
To share with you my staid decorous home.
As wisely had I let a fairy wed me,
Or lured a mermaid from her native foam!

I little knew where frolic Fate was leading,
And can but plead that it was long ago,
When I was sympathetically reading,
The poetry of Edgar Allan Poe.

I felt his Raven's eerie fascination,
And something in me rising seemed to say
(I took it at the time for inspiration),
'Be bold and buy a raven right away.'

I went, I saw, was captivated, bought you,
(Alack! and well-a-day! Or woe is me!)
And to my startled home rejoicing brought you,
To banish gloom and dissipate ennui.

Experience sad, prolonged and comprehensive
Has taught the truth I, fatuous, failed to see,
That one, who temperamentally is pensive,
Must tire in time of tricks and devilry.

Your sins are many, yet I cannot hate you,
Uneasy as I am when you are near;
Today we part, may happier times await you,
And give your talents scope and wider sphere.

My house will then be sober, as it should be,
And I can dream and doze before the fire;
While you, in some far haven where you would be,
May find the kind of home that you desire;

A house with dogs, too small to be afraid of,
Where cats are kept, to petrify and shock,
Where children egg you on and much is made of
The kind of humour that you keep in stock;

Where broken windows long remain unmended,
And larder doors are often left ajar,
Where poultry pens are near and undefended,
Where all the pretty chick-a-biddies are;

Where nothing that you do is deemed intrusive,
And anything you say is gladly heard,
Where everybody likes to be abusive,
And hear his neighbour mimicked by a bird;

Where people at their dinners do not mind you,
But scatter crumbs about them on the floor,
And only think it funny, if they find you
Have pecked the meat about a bit before;

A house with many dark and dusty places,
To hide the stuff you love to loot and store,
Where boots are many—boots with leather laces,
And cushions with interiors to explore;

There take yourself, with all your gifts and graces,
And live an honoured bird for evermore!

RHYME AND REASON

RHYME and Reason, linked together,
  (Much as eggs and bacon are)
Mourn alike a moulting feather,
  And an inauspicious star.

Failed has each to fit the fashion
  Of a hot explosive time.
Reason yields her torch to passion,
  Frenzied singers hoot at rhyme.

Old confections lose their flavour,
  To the emancipated sense,
Obsolete they seem and savour
  Of a doting decadence.

At the name of verse Victorian,
  Upward turns the lyric nose;
'As the dodo or the saurian
  Is it' shrieks impassioned prose!

Once we learnt that lordly reason
  Sat enthroned in mind and brain;
To dispute her sway was treason,
  Now we go to school again,

Learn that instinct, intuition,
  Impulse—call it what you will—
Is the sap that brings fruition,
  And can reason's task fulfil.

Verse, we hear, is shorn of vigour
  By the tinkling torch of rhyme;
Reason cuts a fatuous figure,
  In an anarchistic time.

43

Glorious is the wild-fire burning
   In the dithyrambic breast,
Yet some, not wholly undiscerning,
   Have heard its cracklings unimpressed.

Something of a hope there lingers,
   That passion may not always rage,
That some less saturnalian singers
   May soothe some more saturnian age.

LAMENTATIONS

UNHAPPY flower! that, in another setting,
Had bloomed as violet sweet, as primrose fair,
What careless hand has borne thee here, forgetting
Thou canst not feed on our harsh alien air?
   The smiles of Spring are but as frowns for thee,
   And thy sad Summer shall as Winter be.

Unhappy bird! that in some darkened dwelling,
Sing'st the remembered song of other days,
Round thy lost home the April buds are swelling,
At the warm touch of renovating rays.
   Thy fellows find each his melodious mate,
   Thou sing'st alone, forlorn, disconsolate.

Not yours alone, O hapless bird and flower!
To mourn an altered air, a darkened day.
We share your griefs, who, in Earth's anguished hour,
See youth and youth's fair promise pass away.
   Shadowed by death's all-desolating wing,
   Our hopes have drooped, our hearts have ceased to sing.

TO THE BARNACLE

A Study in Degeneracy

O BARNACLE! My Barnacle! Who would not weep for thee,
Who saw thee in thy jocund youth in ocean frolic free,
And sees thee, in dishonoured age, to rotting timbers cling,
All senses lost, a motionless and miserable thing?

But deep the lesson thou canst teach to men who lightly say,
That he who walks, where Nature leads, is never led astray;
That only Man degenerates, who, mounting o'er the brute,
Has won the power to sink or soar, as his high attribute.

When he is whelmed in gulfs of shame, who might have
    climbed so high,
We say that judgment waits on those who reason's rule defy;
But thou, my Barnacle! art doomed an equal fate to share,
And, looking Nature in the face, we say 'It is not fair.'

NIGHT THOUGHTS

IN those bleak hours that come between
The dead of night and morning star,
Weird sights are by the sleepless seen,
Grim travesties of what has been,
    False visions of things that are.

'Tis then the world shows most forlorn,
And flaws in everything we find;
'Tis then soul-shattering doubts are born,
Then the Night-Huntsman winds his horn,
    And spurs the jaded mind.

45

Then memory unlocks her store,
And brings long-buried griefs to view,
Slights and rebuffs are counted o'er,
And many a barred and bolted door
    Creaks on its hinge anew.

Thoughts that the sunlight laughs away
Throng through the hot distempered brain;
In wild tumultuous disarray,
They swoop like loathsome birds of prey,
    Each with its stab of pain.

Our very hopes are turned to fears,
And, dressed in strange and grisly guise,
Pour horrid warnings in our ears,
Low whispered hints of wasting years,
    And baffled enterprise.

Why did I let the occasion pass,
(We ask) when wisdom bade me buy?
Why did I play the fatuous ass,
And take that last disastrous glass
    Of Brown's old Burgundy?

What made me miss that morning train?
Its punctuality I knew;
To seek the cause is labour vain,
Enough—I lost a chance of gain,
    By that lost interview.

Why did I crack that doubtful joke,
Nor heed my wife's imploring eye?
A shadowy apprehension woke
Within me even as I spoke,
    But did not stop me, why?

Last night—How came I thus to err?
I knew them both and yet I placed
The Dean beside the Dowager—
I might have guessed what would occur,
    When diamond meets with paste!

Why was I weak enough to lend
An ear (and cash) to Smith's request?
My instincts told me it would end
In losing capital and friend,
    As well as interest.

Once more before my face defiles
That preened and fashionable flock,
I see the flickering light of smiles,
Which greets, among the glossy tiles,
    My jaunty billy-cock!

And so the gibbering spectres pass,
The maddening memories come and go;
Like faces in distorting glass,
Neglected duties, errors crass,
    And baulked ambitions flow.

O welcome are the birds that sing,
And tell of wakening day.
Welcome the earliest bells that ring,
Welcome, in short, is anything,
    That hunts these hours away.

47

THE SEDGE AND THE WILLOW

WHAT does the willow sing loud to the sedge,
And the sedge sing low to the willow?
As they sway in the wind at the water's edge,
And bow to the passing billow,
    As they swing together and sing together,
    In a wavering quavering trillo?

They have whispered together for many a year,
When the summer breezes blow;
They have huddled together in frozen fear,
At the snarl of the wintry foe;
    They have shivered together and quivered together,
    As they bent to the falling snow.

They have wept together, in wimples of white,
When the mists on the marsh-lands lie,
Their shadows have met in the westering light,
And danced till the moon was high;
    Then they crept together and slept together,
    To the wavelets' lullaby.

Together they crouch from the north wind's breath,
With its lightning lash of hail;
They have shrunk from its shrivelling touch of death,
Like grain from the thresher's flail.
    They cower together, as they flower together,
    When the balms of Spring prevail.

What should they whisper but words of love,
And of what but of love can they sing,
When, from root to the tremulous tips above,
They are sharers in everything?
    They have grown together, and known together,
    Each joy that the Seasons bring.

'WINTER IN THE LAP OF MAY'

MARCH may wear a scowling face,
Deformed by passions fierce and wild;
We do not look for courtly grace
In surly Winter's wayward child.
     Her sullen airs and gusts of rage
     We pardon for her parentage.

April has atoning tears,
That take the sting from all her bluster.
She frowns, then smiles away our fears;
We love, although we may not trust her.
     With lips that pout and eyes that shine,
     We count her petulance divine.

But May! The enchantress-queen of Spring,
By all her witcheries attended;
E'en at her name our senses sing,
If May be cold, our hopes are ended;
     If love in her be chilled to hate,
     Who shall her guilt extenuate?

Reclaim thine own, dishonoured May!
The traitor winds shall fly before thee;
Cast not thy heritage away,
Of hearts that, as of old, adore thee.
     O mock no more their deep distress,
     Who sigh for thy lost loveliness.

TUTORI DILECTO

OR, THE END OF THE 'LONG'

SHAKE off thy drowsy dull content,
Thine hours of ease are o'er;
Forget the sunny days we spent
On mountain, moor and shore.

Take up again the abandoned task,
And trim the failing fire;
Put up that memory-haunted flask,
Lay by that quaint attire.

A terror be to offending youth,
A rod to them that err;
A teacher of familiar truth,
Or misinterpreter.

Call to thine aid the judgment clear,
By long experience tried,
Which tells thee when to interfere,
And when to stand aside,

The smile that wins a father's heart,
And calms maternal fears,
The frown that makes the guilty start,
And stirs the home of tears.

Once more the athletic fever feel,
Or, feeling failing, feign,
Thy sleek expanding form reveal
In boating guise again.

Thy place resume with those who sit,
Where wine and wisdom flow,
And burnish up the tarnished wit,
That sparkled long ago.

Once more the vacant hour beguile,
With tales you love to tell,
And meet once more the embarrassed smile,
Of those who know them well.

And, when the tedious months have gone,
That sum the toiling year,
Then doff, O doff, the courtly Don,
And let the friend appear.

NOAH AND NOW

WHEN the first anchor fell on Ararat,
And, through the eyes of Noah's congested crew,
Peered hope reborn, aloof the Patriarch sat—
(Earth's earliest ablest Commissariat)
And pondered on the work he had to do.
Problems and difficulties rose to view—
Housing and rationing, schemes of reconstruction,
And how to push things through without a ruction.

He solved them all, at least we may infer
That they were solved, for order lived again.
Ah! would that the inspired interpreter
Had let us know what the solutions were,
That issued from that busy scheming brain
(So taxed he almost wished return of rain).
Of all the wise and holy men of yore,
None could have helped us better now than Noah.

For what he doubtless did we have to do,
Build from the base a world in ruin laid;
Content no more to drift or muddle through;
In dim half-consciousness the old world grew,
But the new world we dream of must be made,
And a new order get itself obeyed;
And now and then a doubt assails us whether
Our inborn gift is putting things together.

If patching, botching, tinkering, talking, spending
Would do the trick, the trick would soon be done;
But digging deep, to hidden roots descending
(I say this at the risk of some offending),
Burning the weeds and letting in the sun,
Is just the sort of thing we loathe and shun.
A principle, in our superior eyes, is
A fad, a whim—our forte is compromises.

Yet glance awhile at what perchance may be,
When the long reign of rapine shall abate,
And the receding waters leave us free,
(Or find us forced as thralls of destiny),
To prop or scrap our worn and battered state,
And write upon a clean but broken slate,
Which of the ways we fondly blindly followed
Will still be there, which will the waves have swallowed?

Will youth be taught what most it needs to know,
Its best and truest self inspired to be,
Or still be choked with lore of long ago?
Will science still be dreaded as a foe,
Unsettling minds too tender to be free?
Will each young climber climb his chosen tree?
Or will there be the same unseemly wrangle,
When truth is viewed from unaccustomed angle?

Will beauty still be spurned, our fields defiled
By pestilential posters puffing pills?
Or will the happy post-diluvian child
Find everywhere some nook of nature wild,
Where it may sport and wander as it wills,
While its young heart with joy and wonder fills,
And, from a home so fair that youth can love it,
Learn something of the Heaven that smiles above it?

Will Faith's dull discords be no longer heard,
When o'er the waste the sun of peace has shone?
Detraction cease, a reconciling word
Pass between Halifax and Hereford,
Sect beckoning sect with an eirenicon?
Or will things go the way that they have gone,
And fiery beams, retricked at Zanzibar,
Flout the mild radiance of Cantuar?

Spirit of Faction! shall thy baleful wing,
Clipped by war's shears, refeather, thy beak and claw
Be buried as of old in everything,
That, whatsoe'er its use or hurt, can bring
Profit and power, to glut thy ravening maw?
And shall our wise, who make or mangle law,
In the old ruts be seen serenely walking,
Convinced that all is well, since all are talking?

Will social broils and bickerings leave a land
Torn by a common grief? Will foe to foe
Stretch o'er the old-time gulf a friendly hand,
Or as opposing armies stiffly stand,
Which pause but to prepare a deadlier blow,
Till all alike are laid in ruin low?
Hope whispers time shall be when men will wonder
That greed had power to tear true hearts asunder.

Will stricken peoples, brooding o'er the past,
Turn on their old oppressors vengeful eyes?
Or will remorse, forgiveness, heal at last
The wounds of loveless ages, and the blast
Of war's wild tempest clear the troubled skies,
And thunder out earth's old antipathies,
That our sons' sons may say, 'They made us free,
Who fell at Europe's dread Thermopylae'?

THE 'ECONOMIC MAN'

A Study in Deductive Political Economy

COMPANION of my wasted youth!
With whom my infant fancy played,
I took thee once for sober truth,
In quaint habiliments arrayed;
    In thy strange 'laws' I loved to trace
    The custom of a vanished race.

And, when maturer thought betrayed
The fact that thou hadst never been,
I let my former fancy fade,
And set thee in a fairer scene,
    In prophet vision saw thee rise,
    In some industrial paradise.

But now, as waking from a trance,
I know thee for the thing thou art,
A sordid hero of romance,
A mummer with a foolish part,
    A joke economists have made,
    A ghost which common sense has laid.

IN AN ANCIENT LIBRARY

TREAD softly here! The dust is deep,
And in the dust long buried, here they sleep,
Who, through the years, their ancient order keep.

In pages spotted o'er with mould,
Some edged with lingering trace of tarnished gold,
The serried tomes their ponderous wisdom hold.

From age-worn lancet overhead,
A little glooming, glimmering light is shed,
And by this light the old-time readers read.

What did they seek, who gathered here,
Where but the bibliomaniac cares to peer,
And the chance-comer scarcely veils his sneer?

And what was found? Did any rise
From these cramped seats, with startled wondering eyes,
Wrapped in the glory of some vast surmise?

Touch lightly! and with reverence due;
'Twas here perchance some darkened spirit drew
The strength to build a broken life anew.

Here lies, in frayed and tattered dress,
What once could fire the blood, or soothe distress,
Or wake the infrequent smiles of loneliness.

Some puzzled sage has hither brought
His tangled thicket of bewildered thought,
And sought with sighs for clue—and vainly sought.

And here some eager questioning mind,
Aflame with zeal some saving truth to find,
Pressed on and left authority behind.

And, to his dire confusion, found,
That he, by solemn vows and orders bound,
Had walked unwitting on forbidden ground.

This portly, cardinal-crested tome,
Like shell that vibrates to the distant foam,
Still holds faint rumblings of the wrath of Rome

Its home-spun neighbour meekly strives
To gather honey from abandoned hives,
And store the sweets of sanctimonious lives.

While here, o'er-sprawled with gloss and note,
With lines deep-scored for pedagogues to quote,
The wind was brewed for many a boisterous throat.

This hide, in rusty ribbons slit,
Still guards its wealth of dull forensic wit,
As when the salt of usage seasoned it.

These shrivelled leaves of old romance
Have made the impetuous novice backward glance,
And change the censer for the pennoned lance.

Here science tried her infant wings,
And mingled dark and subtly-dangerous things
With her devout, inspired imaginings.

To this blurred, mildewed scroll 'twas given,
The sodden dough of life with joy to leaven,
And earth suffuse with rainbow tints of heaven.

Dim visions of approaching light
Have hung and hovered here and, at the sight,
Dust-clouded, thirsting souls have drunk delight

Judge gently! Check the indulgent smile;
Mock not at quaint conceit or pedant style;
But stay and ponder on the past awhile.

Scorn not the stinted light it shed;
The lips, that at this long-dried fountain fed,
Have quivered passion-shaken as they read.

MARCH 29, 1916

WE deemed, mad March! till yesterday,
That, sobered by this year of years,
Thou hadst renounced the War-god's sway,
And, with November's borrowed tears,
Wast weeping, while thy winds forbore to play.

So mild thy mein: thine air so still,
With gloom and sobbing mists oppressed,
That scarce the sprightly daffodil
Stirred on her stem; unused to rest,
She moped and drooped beside the swollen rill.

But now, in fury, like the foe,
That fronts us o'er the Northern sea,
Thou leap'st upon us, blow on blow,
And our dead fields, in maniac glee,
Thou shroudest with the unseasonable snow.

TO OUR SAILORS IN THE
NORTH SEA

DEATH hovers in the deeps of air,
  And lurks in deeps below,
For the hidden snare lies everywhere,
  In the track of a treacherous foe.

The sullen wash of winter wave
  Is ever in your ear,
But, though many a wave be a seaman's grave,
  Your hearts shall be void of fear.

All night the wild wind's wintry breath
  Beats on you fierce and chill,
But, if every breath bore the wings of death,
  Your flag would be flying still.

Far from the thunders of the deep,
  Your foes in harbour lie;
Secure they sleep, while your watch you keep,
  And the angry seas defy.

One hope in your heart has the foeman set,
  One fear that your soul can chill;
The hope he may yet on the seas be met,
  And the fear that he never will.

ABANABEL AND TORQUEMADA

'ROOT OUT! root out the Infidel!
The race accursed, the brood of Hell.'
(From iron lips the mandate fell)
'Scourged from our midst, let none remain,
To taint the air of Catholic Spain,
And ply their godless arts again.'

This was thine hour, Abanabel!
Noblest of the race that fell,
Hope of the sons of Israel.
He fasted, prayed, then sought alone
The bigotry-encircled throne
Of proud Castille and Aragon.
As one who braves the lion's lair,
He sought and found acceptance there,
And stood before the princely pair.
At their feet he pleading fell,
Pleaded wisely and so well,
He stayed awhile the uplifted hand
Of persecuting Ferdinand.
A touch of pity, a gleam of grace,
Found for a moment on his face
An unfamiliar resting place;
While tears of soft contrition fell
From the darkened eyes of Isabel.

Why did high Heaven, that sent them there,
And heard the pleadings of despair,
Call back its gift, reject the prayer?
Idly we ask! To none 'tis given
To probe the dark designs of Heaven.
He back that wave of pity rolled,
Who hardened Pharaoh's heart of old,
And sends the wolf within the fold.

59

A shadow on the presence falls;
A voice the startled court appals,
Like clang of doom in prison walls;
A desolating voice that cried
'Sell ye then thus the Crucified?
Shall the Redeemer twice be sold
To powers unblest for heathen gold?
Ungrateful daughter! faithless son!
Shall the great work, in grace begun,
By human pity be undone?'

Aloft he raised before their face
The symbol of atoning grace—
Reproach of Israel's scattered race.

As from some ice-born arctic blast,
A shudder through the conclave passed;
All shrink before that awful eye,
Which gazed unmoved on agony;
That eye, whose every glance was gloom,
And told of torture and the tomb,
While hope and trembling pity fled,
To join the dying and the dead.

The softened light, that late had shone,
Left the proud eyes of Aragon;
While trouble and confusion fell
On the shrivelled soul of Isabel.

Then those fierce fangs were bared again,
Which tore the quivering heart of Spain,
And made her grace and glory vain.
Faith reeled beneath the sickening spell
Of that grim priest, who tolled the knell
Of thy lost race, Abanabel!

TO GERMANY (1917)

Is there no nook in thy corrupted heart,
No corner of thy misdirected mind,
Where dwells a secret loathing for the part
They chose for thee, who made thee what thou art—
False to thyself, a curse to all thy kind?

We grudged thee not the glory and pride of place
Unquestioned gifts and tireless toil had won;
Outstripped by thee in many a stubborn race,
We praised thy prowess, counted it not disgrace
To learn of thee and do what thou hadst done.

To thee we turned, with homage in our eyes
And raptured ears, when, in their mood profound,
Thy kings of thought, by some august surmise,
Lifted man's vision, when heaven-sent harmonies
Have moved submissive to thy lords of sound.

Our doors stood ever open, welcoming hand
Stretched forth to greet thy restless wandering sons,
No port, no mart, from Cape to Newfoundland,
To intercourse and enterprise was banned,
Our rights were theirs where English order runs.

But lust of dominance, mouthing from the throne,
Met greed and envy muttering from below.
Britain, they said, is spent and overblown,
One crouch, one spring, and all she has we own;
The world is theirs who work her overthrow.

Discordant counsels chill the soul of France,
O'er Russia late the thunder-clouds have rolled,
The Austrian stands alert with lifted lance,
The restless Serb has quailed beneath our glance,
Columbia sits engrossed with gain and gold.

The far Dominions fret and strain the cord,
Binds lusty youth to listless Mother-land;
India but waits the shaking of the sword
To accept with glad acclaim a worthier lord;
Chafed Erin grasps each England-hating hand.

So, many a web of subtle craft and guile
Was woven in secret, deftly veiled from view,
Dark thoughts of treachery lurked beneath the smile
Of him whose specious presence lulled our isle,
O'er whose proud head our flag dishonoured flew.

Then burst the storm, earth reeled before the shock,
A trampled people rose and fought and fell,
Wave following wave broke on the western rock,
Barbarian hordes that ruth and honour mock,
To reach their heaven plied all the arts of Hell.

Still their polluted banner flaunting flies,
While round it all that man can bear is borne,
Still banded Freedom her grim foe defies,
The widow mourns and youth heroic dies,
The sun looks down upon a world forlorn.

The night wears on but, piercing its deepest gloom,
A gleam comes charged with promise of the day,
In serried lines that trace the despot's doom,
The hulls that bear the Western legions loom,
An outraged world has waked and joins the fray.

What thinks she now, who harboured in her breast
Dreams of world-empire? she who, swollen with pride,
Bade her gorged eagles gather to their nest
The spoil of broken peoples, told the oppressed
They sinned resisting, mocked them when they died?

Shall the black shadow of thy shameless deeds
Hunt thee for ever, estrange thee from mankind?
The imperial hopes, on which thy folly feeds,
Blot from thee all man's loftier nature needs,
And leave but a contaminated mind?

Or shall a late compunction turn again
Thy face from him who led thee thus astray?
The chastening hand of loss and grief and pain
Scourge from thy soul its pride and visions vain,
And set thy feet once more upon the upward way?

MY BAROMETER

I own and ever keep beside me,
To cheer me till the storm-clouds pass,
(Though friends, too sadly sane, deride me,)
An old deceitful weather-glass,

Which, like the undaunted feathered singer,
That carols in cannon-quivering air,
Keeps ever an unfaltering finger
Fixed on that soothing legend 'Fair.'

Perchance, like some who should be wiser,
It makes a mock of Natural Law,
Or, like the uncompromising Kaiser,
Holds everything is fair in War.

63

Or, seeing life in blank confusion
And fierce infatuate folly spent,
It turns from fact and courts illusion,
Feigning a fair environment.

Perchance it neither seeks to flatter,
Nor cares to warn when tempests scowl,
But calls to mind the Witches' patter—
Foul is fair and fair is foul.

Or, does it hold the faith 'Pragmatic'
That what is good for man is true?
Or think the Universe is static,
Packed with perfection through and through?

Think everything, whate'er its state is,
In some sublunary phase of thought,
When seen 'sub specie aeternitatis'
Is doing everything it ought?

Perchance, like optimistic Browning,
Whose faith would make a Heaven of Hell,
It sings to a world in deluge drowning—
'God's in His Heaven and all is well!'

While Wisdom to such shifts is driven,
And breathes a fabricated air,
My weather-glass may be forgiven
For always indicating 'Fair.'

And so I frown and feel offended,
When friends, too sadly sober, say
'It's out of order, get it mended,
Or throw the useless thing away!'

THE SECRET OF SUCCESS

A SCRIBE, whose wares were waxing stale,
Whose day had passed its flaming noon,
Dreamed that his gifts might yet avail,
And his confections find a sale,
If, on a large and generous scale,
He did but play the bold buffoon.

The world its favour might renew,
(Such was his reasonable hope,)
If in Convention's face he flew,
And out of all perspective drew,
Looking at everything askew,
Or through an inverted telescope.

So, doubts and scruples cast away,
He aimed at giving people shocks,
Reversed each dogma of the day,
And taught that virtue led astray;
He with hyperboles would play,
And drink the milk of paradox.

So deftly did he play the game,
The critic air was all astir,
And presently he rose to fame,
Built for himself an honoured name,
And—to his own and country's shame—
Was hailed as a philosopher.

And many, following in his tread,
Have learnt the simple truth he taught,
That wisdom standing on its head,
Or moral precepts backward read,
May stand a stinted wit in stead,
And pass with multitudes for thought.

WAR AND WINDERMERE

I WATCH thy wavelets, Windermere!
In sparkles break upon the shore;
Ah! would that they were watching here,
Who loved but may not see thee more.

Whom thou hast seen from Spring to Spring,
Ere a lost world went astray,
Through thy wild woods wandering,
The Spring is here, but where are they?

Youths and maids, a joyous band,
Clambering by thy rocks and rills,
Plucking with an eager hand
Thy now neglected daffodils;

Circling round each wooded isle,
Skirting each enchanted bay,
Resting on the oar awhile,
To watch the coot and dabchick play;

Gazing where the sunset glow
Creeps along thy guardian hills,
Lights and tints the drifted snow
That still their folds and fissures fills;

Lingering till the rocks around
Echo to the owlet's call,
Or give back the muffled sound
Of the wood-bound waterfall;

Listening at the water's edge,
To the moon-loving warbler's song,
As, by banks of reed and sedge,
Silently they drift along.

Where are they who, year by year,
Made their happiest holiday
By thy waters, Windermere!
       Where are they?

       Far away,
Some beneath the sod are lying,
In an unremembered grave,
Day by day are others dying,
In the land they came to save,
       Some beneath the wave.

Others live and broken-hearted
Seek in vain for solace here,
From the loved ones torn and parted,
Who have loved thee, Windermere!

TO THE FOUNDER OF THE
AERATED BREAD CO., LIMITED

PROPHETIC SOUL! Whose searching eye,
Disdainful of Earth's homelier husbandry,
Saw harvests in the over-arching sky;
Prometheus-like, to thee 'twas given
To mingle with the breath of Heaven
The staff of life: on thee descends
The viewless air in dividends.
At thy transfiguring touch, Prophetic Soul!
Glows with ethereal grace the morning roll.
A glory gilds, as of the all-conquering sun,
The subtle essence of the penny bun.

W. E. COLLINS, BISHOP OF GIBRALTAR

DIED AT SEA, 1911. BURIED AT SMYRNA

Not in the shadow of the embattled rock,
That mitred thee, not in thine English home,
O wandering shepherd of a foldless flock!
    Thy feet have ceased to roam.

The crescent waves above thy dying head;
The Aegean spreads and shimmers before thine eyes;
Thine ears are listening for the voice that said—
    'Take up thy bed and rise.'

Thy last of Earth was where Sophia mourns
Her desecration and her ravished cross,
While pagan tinsel mocks her crown of thorns,
    Beside the Bosporos.

There hadst thou found a fit abiding place,
Where East meets West, the Old World fronts the New;
Thy mind from many an age and creed and race
    Its varied wisdom drew.

Greetings have met thee, shaped in many a tongue,
And graced by welcoming flash of Eastern eye,
Thy voice has swelled Nestorian, Syrian, song,
    And Coptic psalmody.

And many a ruined desolated heart,
Has, at thy coming, stirred and pulsed again;
Thy smile has eased the burden, soothed the smart,
    Of penury and pain.

Thou followedst in the track of wandering Paul,
And, frail as he, through suffering didst fulfil
Life's task; in each there triumphed over all
    An indomitable will.

Though round thee float, from mosque and minaret,
The breath of heathen prayer, thy spirit has flown
To where, through storm and toil, thy course was set;
    Reap there what thou hast sown!

AT A FASHIONABLE WATERING-PLACE

As I have known thee once, I see thee still,
    Though, to the outward sense, there lives no more
The quiet hamlet, nestling beneath the hill,
    And downward straggling to a lonely shore.

One moment I, as others, see and hear,
    Then, pier, parade, pavilion, melt away,
The hum of traffic dies, and to my ear
    Comes but a drowsy whisper from the bay.

So, when some traveller, in hot desert sands,
    Or tangled forest, looks upon the face
Of a dead city, musing long he stands,
    And strives to call to life a vanished race.

He peoples there, as I unpeople here,
    He calls a city back, I bid one go;
Each sees the present fade, the past appear,
    One mourns the ebb of life, and one the flow

ODE TO A STEAM-ROLLER IN
THE LAKE DISTRICT

I HEARD thee rolling, as the thunder rolls
Among the mountains, by the misty mere;
Spreading dismay among the simple souls,
Who, seeking peace and beauty, find *thee* here.

I marked thee panting, thine abundant breath
Streams heavenward, battling with the abundant rain,
As life beats back the threatening darts of death,
Or martyred spirit mounts through mists of pain.

No outward grace is thine, the fire that glows
Within thee wakes no answering flame in me;
And yet the lily and the reddening rose
In vital essence are akin to thee.

Why is it that the lily languisheth?
The drooping rose, why withereth she away?
'Tis but the lack of that which gives *thee* breath,
For, without water, what were thou—or they?

No eyes hast thou to mark the beauty by thee,
No temper to be ruffled by the rain;
It is no joy to thee that cattle fly thee;
No rustic admiration makes thee vain.

Yet, when the earth, which trembles at thy tread,
Shall break in blossom with returning spring,
And wind-worn woods rejoice o'er winter dead,
And all around the birds, long silent, sing,

Thy vanished presence shall the tourists bless—
The driven herd, who haunt the hard high road—
Without thee had they sat in deep distress,
As, 'neath the harrow, sits the suffering toad.

AN 'IMPRESSIONIST' PICTURE

CAN it be that meaning lies
Underneath this grim disguise?
Does some shuddering soul of sense—
Some entombed intelligence—
Lurk in this lurid fearsome thing?
Long I lingered wondering,
Hoping that a light would break,
And a slumbering sense awake,
Fearing that what others see
Is for ever hid from me.

Once a gleam of insight came;
'Behold!' I cried, 'a world in flame!
See, amid the central fire,
Chaos, crowned with wild desire;
Gaunt Horror, starting from his lair,
Shakes the lightnings from his hair,
While, clustering round, the powers of Light
Grapple with the Infinite.
Yon towering mass of murk and gloom
Portrays the terrors of the tomb,
And ushers in the Day of Doom;
While that delirious light above
Speaks to our souls of conquering Love.'

Thus I spoke, with kindling eye,
To a critic standing by,
But I could not find support
For my bold and burning thought,

And my smiling mentor said,
Shaking a superior head,
'It is not thus interpreted.'
So the illuminating ray
Quivered, broke and died away:
'Alas!' I cried, in deep distress,
'Art to me is meaningless!'

N.B. A subsequent reference to the catalogue showed that the
picture in question was labelled 'Sheep-washing in the Fens.'

'SELF-REALISATION'

Bid me no more to 'realise
Myself,' whatever that may be;
I know not what the phrase implies,
Which comes so glibly from the wise,
And seems so clear to others' eyes,
        So full of fog to me.

Is 'self' the form I bear about,
The thing I naively know as *I*;
Which eats and golfs and gets the gout,
Attends committees, joins a rout,
Which, briefly, lives, and shuffles out,
        When it is time to die?

Or should we realise alone
The 'self' that scorns the senses' sway,
Which, when to fullest stature grown,
Sits like a seraph on its throne,
Subduing all things to its own,
        Till all have passed away?

And, if the questioned sage replies,
'Each power is good in due degree,
It is the scale that signifies,
In ordered ranks our duties rise,'
One point is left to dim surmise—
     What may that order be?

One argues 'Each with other blends,
A *wider* self within us lies,
And far that wider self extends,
To wife and children, foes and friends,
And ever-widening, only ends,
     Where all division dies.

'When thus the many, fused in one,
Have left the narrower selves behind,
Our *real* existence has begun,
The fight is fought, the victory won,
And all that lives beneath the sun,
     May be oneself defined.'

Vain words, that soothe the pedant ear,
But leave us where we stood before,
Not thus our doubts will disappear,
We end with no solution near;
We hoped for help and guidance clear,
     And have—one phrase the more!

THE CRY OF THE CRICKETER

(When Golf came south)

'PROCUL, O PROCUL ESTE PROFANI!'

GOLF is a noxious weed,
Transplanted here,
From that bleak barren land beyond the Tweed,
To kilted Scots so dear.

Cease, Vandals, Goths and Huns,
This game unblest,
Or teach it to your own dull, breechless sons,
And let our land have rest.

No more our tongue defile,
With words uncouth,
No longer from their native sports beguile
Our unoffending youth.

Your graceless caddies call,
And bid them pack,
Rebuild your bunkers where dark Hadrian's wall
Kept like barbarians back.

There munch your native oats,
Your whisky quaff,
Play your dull game from Tweed to John o' Groat's
While saner Southrons laugh.

74

A QUESTION OF PRECEDENCE

THE SUPRA-LIMINAL AND THE SUB-LIMINAL SELF

I. THE SUPRA-LIMINAL (CONSCIOUS) SELF

WE who share the common fate,
And a common burden bear,
Joint upholders of one state,
Make of life division fair.
  We are not as some have seen us,
  Discord never comes between us;
  Thou art means, and I am end;
  Hail my humble, helpful friend!

Mine the privilege to know
All the glories life can give,
Thine to labour down below,
Toiling that the soul may live.
  I the ship of life am steering,
  Thou below art engineering.
  Mine the end that governs all,
  Thine the means mechanical.

Inspiration streams to me,
From the light that burns above;
Half-formed thoughts I fling to thee,
In my condescending love.
  Everything that I am sending,
  Thou art weaving, patching, mending,
  Fashioning habits fit to wear
  In my conscious upper air.

75

II. THE SUB-LIMINAL SELF

If thou wouldst indeed have peace,
In the common life we share,
Let thy condescensions cease,
Drop that supercilious air!
    Boast no more of thy dominion,
    Preen no more thy moulting pinion,
    Know—thy former view reversed—
    Thou art last and I am first!

Thine are but the gleams that pass,
Flickering lights, that come and go,
Bright reflections in a glass
Of reality below.
    For, in spite of outward seeming,
    I am acting, thou art dreaming,
    And life's central glories shine
    In a region wholly mine.

Thoughts that rise and flash in thee,
In thy rapt exalted hour,
Thy presumption takes to be
Proofs of independent power.
    They are but the spray that ever
    Rises from the caverned river,
    Which, moving towards the eternal sea,
    Wanders awhile on earth with me.

THIRLMERE WATERWORKS

OR, 'MANCHESTERISMUS'

WITH suppliant air she came to plead
For thirsting souls beneath her sway;
We had compassion on her need,
And let her bear our springs away.
And so, through prisoning pipes and caverns long,
She led them, silencing the streamlet's song.

We bore that, through the toiling years,
Our pleasant hills were seamed and scarred;
We strove to calm artistic fears,
And smooth the plumes of ruffled bard;
We trusted to the pledges given by her;
We did not know thee then, false Manchester!

She promised, did we let her take
Our waters hence, her care should be,
To guard, around her larger lake,
The beauties thousands flocked to see.
We lent a readier ear, who long had known
Her creed of 'laissez faire' or 'let alone.'

Now, false to creed and pledges given,
Rejecting Nature's kindly aid,
She makes her artificial heaven,
In place of that which God had made;
With alien blocks of red and gates of blue,
She decorates the roads—*improves* the view!

A forest, latest here that clings
To mountain side, she tears away;
'It does not harmonise with things
Around'—the civic sages say.
Each mossy stone she scrapes with jealous care,
Lest Nature in her work should claim a share.

'WHITE-WASH'

(As applied by certain historians)

NOT ours to view with cold accusing eyes
The frailties of monarchs or of men;
If down in dust a reputation lies,
'Tis ours to set it on its feet again.
    If mercy is above the sceptred sway,
    Shall truth presume to stand in mercy's way?

And so we take our way across the ages,
Lightening the shadows, laying on the paint;
And; when we come to dark dishonouring pages,
Which say that men are vile, we say 'they ain't.'
    To whiten Whigs we go to Lord Macaulay,
    For Revolutionists to Viscount Morley.

Full many an ancient name defaced and tarnished
Has come to us with orders to repair,
Which now shines forth retouched and brightly varnished,
A sight to make contemporaries stare.
    In fact, unless we wrote their names below them,
    The very mothers of them would not know them.

To test our skill—Indulgent and forgiving
Was the Eighth Henry to his friends and wives,
If he had thought that they were worth the living,
He would not, for the world, have ta'en their lives.
    He could not make them wise or great or good,
    And so he simply did the best he could.

And even Nero made a good beginning,
And, but for Providence which shapes our ends,
Had ended well; more sinned against than sinning,
Fate gave him a philosopher for friend,
    And, ere he put in practice half he learnt,
    He burnt his city (Rome was better burnt).

If Timour ran amok in sundry places,
(He slew two million men or more, 'tis said,)
They all belonged to those inferior races,
Which many tell us now are better dead.
    He faced the Eugenic problem of his day,
    And solved it in his own emphatic way.

If John was bad, his age was little better,
He pleased himself, as others did and do,
And, when he died, all England was his debtor,
If any page of history is true;
    If he had lived a saint, or died a martyr,
    Where in the world were England's Magna Carta?

Pope Alexander Borgia gave us trouble,
His reputation was so badly blown,
But reputation—mark you—is a bubble,
And justice bids us judge him not alone;
    Take him together with his son and daughter,
    And then his evil deeds we write in water.

Turn to the case of Catherine the Second,
Theodora, Messalina, judge the three
Imperial dames together; each was reckoned
To be 'no better than she ought to be.'
     Take the charge strictly, who could stand the test?
     For who can e'er be better than the best?

You guess, of course, and hardly need to ask it,
Our treatment of the injured Queen of Scots.
We brush aside the compromising casket,
And show her reputation free from spots.
     She was a simple soul, who lightly drew her breath,
     And talked no scandal about great Elizabeth.

And though great Bonaparte was wont to be
A little cold and callous now and then,
As when he softly murmured 'What to me
The lives of half a million of men?'
     He showed another spirit when, at home,
     He rocked the cradle of the King of Rome.

And so of all the rest, upon enquiry,
There's something good to say of every one;
If Pepys was frail, he wrote a charming diary,
Oates liked his glass and Wilkes disliked a dun.
     We hope, with reasonable time and care,
     To whiten Jeffreys, Kirke and Robespierre.

THE GREEN CATERPILLAR

O, what did they do at Dodona?
What did the Dodonians do?
(I ask as the ignorant owner
  Of oaks not a few,)

When the hosts of the green caterpillars
Invaded their sacred domain?
Did they call in a posse of millers,
  To grind them like grain,

And bake them for feasts sacrificial,
Or spread them like butter on bread,
Or extract from them oil beneficial,
  To the hair of the head?

Were they used on the farms for manuring,
Or for feeding of fowls or of pigs,
Or by doctors and barbers for curing,
  And powdering wigs?

Whatever their use or their uses,
When up they had given the ghost,
What we want is the way that reduces
  Their number the most.

And, if we're unable to find it,
If no remedy seems to be known,
We must make up our minds not to mind it,
  And leave them alone.

But, what did they do at Dodona?
I am sure, if their story is true,
They could give to the oak and its owner,
  A wrinkle or two.

ROADSIDE ADVERTISEMENTS

UNTOUCHED by foe's defiling feet
Our land has been and still shall be.
Here heaven-born freedom stoops to greet
Earth's beauties spreading till they meet
And shimmer with the shimmering sea.

Vain boast! A meaner, greedier foe
Than ever struck at England's weal,
With impious desecrating blow,
Has dared to lay her beauty low,
And spurn it with a huckster's heel.

He stamps on Nature's living face
The impress of a jaunty lie,
Turning her smile to his grimace,
And sullying every tender grace,
To win some fool's approving eye.

Where hung but clustering blooms, today
His lying legend blinks and stares;
By many an ancient winding way,
And lane where lovers love to stray,
He vaunts his despicable wares.

By moorland, marsh and mountain side,
The beauty-blasting sign is seen;
It gleams reflected in the tide,
Where reed-bound rivers dream and glide,
It gapes on every village green.

Before these baleful, basilisk eyes,
Lit by dull fires of greed and gain,
Earth's beauty sickens, droops and dies,
And far affronted Nature flies,
To save her soul and ease her pain.

At honour's call, we fearless stand,
To front a tyrant's grim array,
Yet may not lift indignant hand,
To scourge these spoilers of our land,
And hunt our English Huns away.

TO COUNT ZEPPELIN (1915)

BENEATH the war-god's furious feet,
Earth cowers in fear and pain;
His trumpets never sound retreat,
Her cries for peace are vain.

Long has he held dominion wide,
O'er shuddering earth and sea;
One element alone defied
His sin-born sovereignty.

And now he rides the afflicted air,
And owes that realm to thee,
Who bore his blood-stained banner there,
And shared his impious glee.

To thee, as to some vengeful fate,
The 'War-lord' frowning turned,
When his low smouldering fires of hate
With new-fed fury burned.

His legions long, with angered eyes,
Had glowered across the sea,
Where, girt by many a squadron, lies
The land of liberty.

Could but those baffling waves be passed,
That shrouded shore be won,
The longed-for 'Day' might dawn at last,
And Britain's race be run.

The fire of heaven Prometheus brought
To earth was kindly given,
With deadlier purpose thou hast wrought,
To raise earth's fire to heaven.

Thine are the shadowy forms that flit
By night and shun the day;
And thine the baleful fires that lit
The raider's lawless way.

O'er homes of drowsy peace they passed,
Their seeds of death to sow;
They rode exulting on the blast,
And hurled their bolts below.

Till man repents and, steeped in shame,
Turns from his hate and sin,
His frenzied sons shall vaunt thy fame,
And hail Count Zeppelin.

SALMO 'FONTINALIS'

BY PISCATOR PEDANTICUS

FONTINALIS! daintiest, brightest
Of the tribe 'Salmonidae,'
For the fight thou gamely fightest,
I have loved and honoured thee.

'Salmo Salar' (lordly Salmon)
Leaps, beyond my purse and sphere,
For the pampered son of Mammon,
And the plutocratic peer.

But of humbler fishes there is
None that makes so brave a show,
What is 'Tinca (tench) Vulgaris,'
Or Carp ('Cyprinus Carpio')?

'Rutilus Leuciscus' (Roach) is
Fair to see and hard to hook,
But nowhere near thee it approaches;
Ask the angler! ask the cook!

'Tis but the vulgar mindless rabble
Or breechless youth can count it bliss
For the Common Perch to dabble,
('Perca Fluviatilis').

Moody-minded men may sit for
Hours nodding o'er their lure,
Muddy fishes catching, fit for
(Frankly) nothing but manure.

Let the fog-befuddled farmer,
Coughing by his oozy stream,
Boast of his 'Abramis Brama,'
Known (vulgariter) as Bream.

Let the bog-bound Fenman fish for
'Esox Lucius' in the Fens;
That is not what he should wish for,
Who is 'Homo Sapiens.'

None can match thee, 'Fontinalis'!
Though the years ('labuntur') go,
I shall catch thee, till the veil is
Dropped on everything below.

TO THE EAST

THOUGHT-BURDENED East! East of the brooding brow!
Not the wide-rolling wonder of the sea,
Nor midnight heaven can steep man's soul as thou,
In awe and deep abiding mystery.

Thine are Aurora's blushes, thine the light
That trembles in the track of Lucifer,
But radiance purer, more divinely bright,
Has streamed through thee, high Heaven's interpreter.

From thee came forth priest, prophet, sage and seer,
The thundered dooms of Sinai, wisdom hid
In parable and myth, truth sifted clear
In Porch, and pondered by the Pyramid.

Gautama, Zoroaster, Mahomet,
Confucius, these were thine, and thine was He,
Whose light shall shine when every sun has set,
And time has passed into eternity.

Age after age illumination came,
The warning voices spoke, new seed was sown,
Culture on culture rose and passed in flame,
Faith followed faith on a precarious throne.

Thick darkness fell on Tyre and Babylon,
The desert sands have closed on Nineveh,
Thebes, Memphis and Palmyra, all are gone,
Antioch and Alexandria, what are they?

They followed wandering fires which led astray,
Piled pomp on pomp, fed fat each earth-born lust;
Let pride and pampered passion have their way,
Till all their domination died in dust.

The beaconing lights, thou hadst exalted high,
Waxed dim, men scorned the glories of the mind;
Thy fairest fields in desolation lie,
Thy fruits are cast upon the desert wind.

Contention tore man's heart, and seared his soul,
The heavenly vision passed beyond his ken,
Till, worn and spent, he heard the chariot roll,
The trampling feet of Turk and Saracen.

What of the West, where poised the balance hangs?
Shall equal folly bring an equal fate?
Shall she escape the soul-devouring fangs,
Or, in like ruin, dissolve, disintegrate?

Her yearning gaze was once upon the East,
And from the East may yet salvation come,
To uplift mankind once more above the beast,
And fan the waning fires of Christendom.

If sap still move in that fructiferous tree,
Whose roots lie deep in India's soulful soil,
O may some quickening shoot engrafted be
On our worn trunk, shaken by vast turmoil.

TO THE 'TERRITORIALS' IN THE TRENCHES (1915)

WHAT brings ye here, that live among the dying,
Soon haply to be numbered with the dead?
What holds ye here and keeps your banner flying?
Though all life's joys have flown, ye have not fled.
    Lashed by the storm, by frost and fire assailed,
    Racked by this whirlwind war, your hearts have never
        quailed.

The gilded pomp of war, the plumed array
Of gleaming chivalry, the pageant throng,
Soul-moving music—all has passed away
That made war glitter in the poet's song.
    Yet here ye come, here ye undaunted stay,
    Where, after hideous night, breaks yet more hideous day

Ye were not bred to war; from many a home
Of peace, embowered cottage, feudal hall,
And calm sequestered college, do ye come;
Ye saw a vision and ye heard a call.
    Not lured by gain: not driven by harsh command;
    Ye sought this bleak, sad, desolated land.

Ye saw an old and blameless people rise,
To front the oppressor, saw them overthrown;
Their burning homes shone in their burning eyes,
Ye caught the fire and made their wrongs your own;
    The call of honour sounded o'er the sea,
    Mindful of plighted faith, ye swore to set them free.

Fight on! brave hearts, and faint not, far above,
The star of peace hangs dim, but soon shall glow
And brighten with returning light of love,
Quenching the baleful beams of war and woe.
  Though days of straining horror, nights of pain
  Be yours, fight on! Ye shall not fight in vain.

AFTER THE WAR

IF troubled ether, agitated air,
Can make a sunset or a symphony;
If soil most foul can turn to flower most fair,
And order on disorder everywhere
Must mount, and error live ere truth can be,

O then may hope be ours that, through the gloom
Of war and war's wide-wasting anarchy,
Some spirit of health may rise from out the tomb
Of our dead past: some flowers of grace may bloom,
That grew not in earth's old aridity.

With such a faith we prop our battered state,
And search our ruined fields for golden grain,
And, mid the clash of warring empires, wait,
As they who watch to see the storm abate,
And the glad sunshine flood God's earth again.

Misled no more by pride that will not learn,
We cast around our eager altered eyes,
And, with flushed brows and thoughts that flash and burn,
With tremulous fears and fevered hopes, we turn
To scan the horizon for this sun's uprise.

What mists of error may its beams dispel!
The foul miasma of a poisoned past,
Which wrapped our isle in stifling fumes of Hell,
And laid on liberty its deadening spell,
Binding our souls in sordid fetters fast.

O! May it shine on homes made meet to be
The soil from which our native valour springs,
Where love may mate with beauty, toil with glee,
And life be lived in rounded symmetry,
Crowned with the peace that freedom only brings.

May those who, linked as brothers, faced the foe,
As brothers be, when war has passed away,
Building no more their weal on others' woe,
And finding in their hearts' more generous glow
The recompense for many a dolorous day.

May eyes that open to that morning's light
See knowledge spread like some illumined sea,
And ears be tuned to catch and read aright,
With ever deepening wonder and delight,
The heavenly note in earth's great symphony.

Take not from hearts, by fierce affliction torn,
Their last best hope that what has been may be
The passing of a world misused outworn,
The dark dread hour that comes before the dawn,
The death of strife and birth of harmony.

'PRO PATRIA' VERSUS 'DULCE ET DECORUM'

(*The Plaintiff was 'non-suited'*)

THERE'S a sort of satisfaction when you've had a nasty blow,
    In telling other people all about it,
So I'm setting down in writing what I think you ought to know,
    And hope to get your sympathy, but doubt it!

It's the duty of the moment—so our legislators say—
    To save your ready money, not to spend it:
To wear your hat or coat until it moulders in decay,
    And not to buy another, but to mend it.

So, in frayed and tattered raiment, I compelled myself to go,
    And schooled myself to think it did not matter,
If a farmer asked me coaxingly to stop and scare the crow,
    Or a townsman lavished praises on my hatter.

This patriotic virtue may be pleasing to the gods,
    Who look beneath the act to the intention;
But I grieve to say, when Virtue and Convention are at odds,
    You may safely put your money on Convention.

For I woke and found one morning that my many-seasoned suit
    Had been ravished from me—gone, I fear, for ever,
And a new one substituted, which has poisoned at the root
    All my patriotic virtuous endeavour!

EVOLUTION

(Without tears)

WHEN Nature set herself to work, she did it in a way,
Which seems a little odd to us, who order things today.
She did not think the matter out, or draw up any plan,
But she started in a hurry and she reasoned as she ran,
With the confident assurance of an optimistic man.
Her misses were so many and her hits so very few,
That the wonder is she ever had the luck to muddle through;
But she hadn't any scruples and she never made a fuss,
If the way in front was blocked she tried a circumbendibus.

She churned quiescent ether up and stepped aside to see
Existence oozing slowing from potentiality,
And an integrating order stir the misty bounds of space,
So she lashed about her lustily, to quicken up the pace,
With a smile of satisfaction on her interesting face.

She mixed a lot of matter with the thing we know as life,
And, to make her creatures livelier, she set them all at strife—
Some were fighting for a dinner, others fighting for a wife—
And the one that ate the other was the one she counted 'fit,'
Or, to put it scientifically, she 'selected' it.
Strange forms of life came bubbling up, with eager wondering
  eyes,
Each with its little aptitudes, its faint antipathies.
She sorted them and sifted them, in ocean, earth and air,
And she filled the nooks and crannies with the stuff she had
  to spare,
And the conscientious entity, that did not care to fight,
Had to vanish from existence, or become a parasite.

92

There were large and lumpish lizards, in that old and foolish
   time,
Which led a dull existence in a sort of slushy slime;
Though some had bodies bigger than the biggest London 'bus.
They were mostly inoffensive, being graminivorous.
With the maximum of body went the minimum of mind,
When the rest were romping forward, they came rumbling on
   behind.
They may pass as early efforts, but they did not run to brain,
So Nature swept them all away and set to work again.
The whale was in the water once, and once upon the shore,
And now its gone to sea again—we trust for evermore.

And other clumsy creatures came, that did not come to stay;
They were willing to develop, but they could not find the way.
The ones we see around us are the ones that guessed the game,
They have found the place they wanted, so they mostly keep
   the same,
Being tired of progressing and indifferent to fame.

Next she took a lively lizard, and its faint ambition stirred,
Till it mounted in the heavens, as a silly sort of bird;
Though it could not boast of beauty, and it did not care to
   sing,
In the eye of Evolution its an interesting thing,
The doyen of the tuneful race that live upon the wing.

And so creation shambled on, and, as the ages went,
Each saw some new departure made, some fresh experiment.
There were many ghastly failures, like the octopus and shark,
Suggesting inexperience, or groping in the dark,
Or the coarser kind of joking, which the vulgar call a 'lark.'
But do not let us look at life, like pessimists, and say,
It's a boggled, bungled business and had better pass away.

93

We should not pitch our airy hopes unreasonably high,
Or judge our fellow-creatures with too critical an eye.
The very worst among us may be better by and by.

Well, Nature looked upon her work with pardonable pride,
There was much that did her credit, still she was not satisfied.
She was tired of making monsters like the hippopotamus,
So she fixed her aim on higher game and set to work on us.

The result was disappointing for, in attitude and shape,
We were very little better than the ordinary ape;
But she straightened up the forehead, and she modified the
      thumb,
And then she smiled contented, for she knew the rest would
      come,
And let us spin the top ourselves and try to make it hum.

And so it came to pass that, after many many days,
There were lots of funny men about, with lots of funny ways;
They were very fierce and ugly, and their views were very
      short,
But they wanted to be better, and were willing to be taught,
Having morals in the making, even manners—of a sort.
Their brains kept growing bigger and they learnt a trick or
      two
(They were eating one another then, but found it didn't do).
They learnt the use of weapons, of the boomerang and bow,
They mounted on a horse and learnt the way to make him go.
After long dyspeptic ages they discovered it was best
To put food upon the fire, to help it to digest.
Though their matrimonial matters were a common source of
      strife,
They came to see the value of the woman as a wife.

When conversation languished, from the lack of proper signs,
A language was constructed, though on very simple lines.
They did not care for grammar, and they thought it early yet,
To tabulate the parts of speech, or start an alphabet.

They tried to be religious, though their attitude was odd
To the gusty personality they fancied as a god.
Their views were rudimentary in many other ways,
But they slowly sifted out their most unedifying traits,
And found 'adaptability' to be the thing that pays.
With a caution most commendable, when a custom ceased to fit,
They said 'We do not alter, but we re-interpret it'
(Unconsciously foreshadowing our own forensic wit).
Still they fought with one another, till, as brains and morals
        grew,
And men distinguished what they did from what they ought
        to do,
They fought about the meaning of the Beautiful, the True,
And vexed their souls with problems which we cannot solve
        today,
Though we think in many matters we have found a better way.

There are many here among us who will argue that a fight
Is the only way to settle if a thing is wrong or right.
Though life is mostly struggle, it does not do to say
That ways which told in days of old will work as well today.
We have learnt cooperation and the law of give and take,
And we spend a little trouble for another person's sake.
Though fighting has its uses, it is better, in the end,
To give up making enemies, and try to make a friend.
The race that saunters onwards, with no sweat upon its brow,
Leads a slovenly existence, and is better for a row;
But the race that lives for nothing but the rapture of the strife,
Pays a lot of ready money for an agitated life.

> ' I have a gentil cok,
> Croweth me day.'

HENCE! worthy fowl! thy duty done—
To usher in the dawning day,
And rouse from sleep the indignant sun—
Accept our grateful thanks and run
                    Away!

And, if thou carest for length of days,
Be not, O blessed bird! a bore.
Reiteration rarely pays,
The true musician seldom says
                    'Encore.'

Clothed in thy self-importance, go!
A lustier braggart never crew;
Let all the world thy prescience know,
I only say a single crow
                    Will do.

If still thou sound'st thy clarion clear,
And think'st my warning to defy,
Thy fate will be, O dear! O dear!
(If I have any influence here)
                    To die!

TO A HERON

Heron! All my hints unheeding,
(All my imprecations vain,)
On my fish I find thee feeding,
Feeding on my fish again!
I thy horoscope am reading,
And thy star is on the wane.
        Brother fisher! Former friend!
        Ponder on thy latter end!

Long thy grace and beauty pleaded;
When I doomed thee, Dear, to die,
Something inly interceded,
And I put my purpose by.
        Go! and all thy sins are pardoned,
        Stay not till my heart is hardened.

Hie thee to the rippled sand,
By the shallow, ebbing sea;
There thy long-legged brethren stand—
A solemn meditative band,
Like some grave Presbyt'ry—
        Share heronian bliss with them,
        Build there thy New Jerusalem!

There are fishes fatter far
Than my 'fontinalis' are,
And no foes to fear;
Here, in spite of all thy cunning,
Swift the sands of life are running,
And the bitter end is near.

Trust no more to my relenting,
Long the sentence was deferred,
Grace was given for repenting,
Not to stay the circumventing
Of a contumacious bird!

Vain the warning! and the dawning
Of the doleful day is here.
Hast thou, Heron, no foreboding,
While the lethal gun is loading,
And the gunner drawing near?

I salute thee, ere I shoot thee,
(Sentimental fratricide!)
As Othello (foolish fellow!)
Did when Desdemona died.

Will tomorrow bring me sorrow?
Shall I feel a 'Hun'?
Will a long remorse awaken,
For the life that I have taken,
And my very soul be shaken
By the deed that I have done?

When the Autumn mists are falling,
In the hollows dank and dree,
Shall I hear,—O thought appalling!—
Thine unquiet spirit calling
Curses down on me?
As, in accents faint and airy,
Calls the cattle-calling Mary,
On the dreary sands of Dee.

Nearer comes thy floating figure,
(May thy sinful soul have rest!)
Nearer yet and bulking bigger,
Now to pull the fatal trigger!
It is done and—'Well, I'm blest!!!'

A SERENE OLD AGE

WHEN life has ebbed from flower and fruit,
And her cast robes in tatters lie,
She but retires within the root,
And mocks at Winter blustering by;
    Nor doubts each energy withdrawn
    Will wake to greet a kindlier dawn.

So, in some soft and scented isle,
Set in the foam of thundering seas,
The battered wanderer rests awhile,
And dreams and wakes in languorous ease;
    Yet, as he counts his perils o'er,
    He sighs and inly yearns for more.

Freed from the loosening coils of sense,
The weary straining of the will,
We hail the Powers that draw us hence,
And bid them all their task fulfil;
    Yet pray, if aught that dies return,
    We still may strive and still may learn.

TO THE 'PATRIARCH'

A Study in Anthropology

(The Patriarchal Theory of the origin of political society
was supported by Sir Henry Maine and attacked by J. F.
and D. McLennan.)

THY place was high among the great,
Who bore of old unquestioned sway,
But, hoary chief! Balshazzar's fate—
Despair and death—is thine today,
  For men have risen who dare to doubt,
  And say that they have found thee out.

Thy throne and its foundations shook,
When, like the writing on the wall,
Two bold bad brothers wrote a book,
To prove you never lived at all.
  They say that earth's primaeval lord,
  Is but a venerable fraud.

They trod the weary road again,
Which led us once—we thought—to thee;
They laughed to scorn our master—Maine,
Who strove for thy supremacy,
  And raised, although her faults they own,
  The 'Mutter'[1] to thy vacant throne.

In her they hail the source of race,
Of tribal bonds in peace and war,
From her the devious line they trace,
Which leads to ordered life and law,
  And coldly add they fail to see,
  What further need there is of thee.

[1] 'Mutterrecht' theory.

'WHY THESE WEEPS'

'I may add that it is only with the deepest regret and with death in his soul that the Kaiser proceeds to these extremities.'
(Statement of German Official)

Weep on! thou crowned crocodile;
Weep, as thou wept'st o'er lost Louvain.
Bedew thy soul with tears awhile,
Then to thy hellish tasks again.

In ' holy wrath,' with hymns of hate,
Fill the wide world with pain and woe;
Enslave, deport, asphyxiate,
Then bid the tear-fed fountain flow.

Sow death along the travelled deep,
And wing it through the wintry skies,
To fall where babes and children sleep,
Then weep to hear the mothers' cries.

Weep, as they wept in days of old,
Who bade the martyr 'go in peace,'
To where the torturing flames enfold,
Long ere they grant the soul release.

He who first urged the tyrant's plea,
Had tears like thine within his eyes,
When sighing 'sad necessity,'
He broke the peace of Paradise.

Bid the chill waves of winter roll
O'er peaceful toilers of the sea,
And then, with death within thy soul,
Weep for man's inhumanity.

Weep most for those who rudely dare
At thy fantastic tears to smile;
Thy heart is cold as liquid air,
Weep on, thou kingly crocodile!

LOST LANDS REVISITED

As fair a wood may wave, and wave for me,
Another streamlet as melodious fall,
As these which, waving, murmuring, here I see,
    And once my own could call.

My own by double title, law and love,
A love deep-rooted as my sturdiest tree,
As constant as yon star, that keeps above
    Its course eternally.

But never more shall woodland, glen or stream
Bring to my soul the peace that these have brought,
Restore the joys of which I nightly dream,
    Or teach what these have taught.

There is no path in this far-spreading wood,
But I have made it wander to my will;
No rock, no stone, on which I have not stood,
    By this meandering rill.

For me the larches shook their tasselled tops,
The birches quivered, like a rippling sea;
For me the hyacinth blossomed in the copse,
    And wood-anemone.

I knew alone, perchance alone I know,
The hidden source of this o'er-hazelled spring,
Set round with mossy stones—I ranged them so—
    Like to a fairies' ring.

Yon moorland tarn, that in the distance glows,
With the last flush of the evening's dying red,
Was mine; its waters at my bidding rose
    From out their peaty bed.

In this deep dell another's eyes may peer,
And here another kneel as I have knelt,
To greet the earliest primrose of the year,
    And feel as I have felt.

Yet still for me the peat-brown waters shine,
The streamlet falls, light glistens on flower and tree;
Let others own! all are in memory mine,
    And evermore shall be.

THE TREE OF LIFE

I STOOD in dream where Life's far-shadowing tree,
   On the drear waste that bounds all being, grows;
Its roots their sustenance draw from that dread sea,
   Whose source and depth and issue no man knows.

I watched Life's teeming myriads wake and climb,
   In wide-eyed wonder at their differing ways,
Some perished ere they left the encircling slime,
   Scarce saw the sun, or felt his quickening rays.

Some strove and prospered, thrusting their fellows back,
   And with glad steps sped upward towards the light;
Each by some inward impulse chose its track,
   Or outward urge; some gloried in the fight,

While others, finding smooth environment,
   Let the fierce fires of action fail and die,
Wrapped in cold lethargy or dull content,
   They heeded not the hosts that passed them by.

Some, more adventurous, pushed their blundering way
   To the far limits of some lateral bough,
And there they stopped, and must for ever stay,
   No second choice Life's guardian Powers allow.

And some there were that, rising, ever saw
   A beckoning hand which bade them further rise,
Till mastering mind loosed the dull grip of law,
   And light from heaven streamed through man's opening
      eyes.

Few were there favoured thus, and these alas!
  Full oft their fellows' fortunes imitate;
Slothful or blind they pause where they might pass,
  Spurn their best gifts, turn new-born love to hate.

Yet are there ever some that steadfast stand
  When others fall, press forward when they stay,
Who grasp occasion with unfaltering hand,
  And mount exulting towards eternal day.

WAR (1917)

NOT yet it passes! still the cloud
Hangs darkly shadowing every heart;
Tired Earth has changed her vesture for a shroud,
And the red shambles stand, where stood the mart.
    Life is half death and everywhere is mourning,
    The future dim, of menace full and warning.

With labouring breath, we pant and strain,
To where, in distance faint and far,
The sunlit uplands shimmer above the plain,
The abode of Peace, where all our longings are.
    Through dark ravines and gloomy forest groping,
    Onward we press, enduring, fainting, hoping.

If we those longed-for heights should win,
And rest our forces worn and spent,
Will there a new and nobler life begin,
Or the old return, untamed impenitent?
    Will there be home, joy, peace and sound of singing,
    Or but a hive distracted, buzzing, stinging?

THE GIANT OCTOPUS

FAR down in dark abysmal deeps,
Unpierced by mortal eyes,
Where everlasting silence sleeps,
The unshapen horror lies.

No form that frenzied fear can take,
Or fevered fancy feign,
A deadlier loathing can awake,
Or wilder thoughts unchain.

The scaly serpent's venomed head,
And dull malignant eye,
Stir not such sickening sense of dread,
Such dreams of devilry.

The fabled dragon's fiery breath,
The basilisk's stony glare,
Are not more eloquent of death,
Than what lies watching there.

The soul that nursed immortal hate,
And knew eternal pain,
Might such a form reanimate,
And challenge heaven again.

Can aught that springs from Power above—
Some cankered shoot of mind,
Or wildered ray of wandering love—
In that fell form be shrined?

Or lives such worth in life alone,
Howe'er ignobly pent,
That its mere presence can atone
For foul embodiment?

RED RAPTURE

O HAD I Ariel's harp, Apollo's lute,
The Triton's horn, or reedy pipe of Pan,
Mad Nero's fiddle, forceful Frederick's flute,
    Or any instrument abused by man,
I should be piping, puffing, twanging, stringing, strumming,
To celebrate the glorious time that's coming.

But as I scarce know one note from another,
    And can but wildly guess at tune or time,
And yet disdain my rapturous mood to smother,
    It follows that I give it vent in rhyme;
Let others trumpet out their Marseillaises,
I sit and sing—The old world's gone to blazes!

Look where a new and brighter orb emerges,
    Rising like Aphrodite in her shell,
Or as Poseidon, when above the surges
    He rose and winked, to show that all was well.
That orb is ours, to mould it to our pattern,
The old gods sink below, to sulk with Saturn.

Who has not felt the rapture of creation,
    And known the joy of blowing things to bits?
Pleasant it is to reconstruct a nation,
    And pleasant too is giving people fits.
When these emotions meet, the most censorious
Must melt and own the situation's glorious.

O Britain! Britain! when from sea to sea
    Thou liest lapped in joys that now begin,
Transformed, transfused, transfigured shalt thou be
    Thy visage graced by a perennial grin,
Let me unveil that face, reveal those features,
To inform and edify our fellow-creatures.

Corn shall be grown on every breezy height,
And rustle mid the shingle of the shore;
Foxes and pheasants shall be shot at sight,
Parks, poachers, prosecutors be no more;
Each marsh and swamp be drained and fit to dwell in,
While forests wave on Snowdon and Helvellyn.

The very climate shall relax its rigour,
Fogs shall disperse and regulated rain
Come when we call it, crops shall all be bigger,
And loss no longer dog the heels of gain;
Love, peace, contentment all our ills shall banish;
Disease shall cure itself, and doctors vanish.

Ye ask for land—Take what ye want and till it,
And pay for rent a peppercorn a year.
Your glass is empty—Publicans shall fill it,
With liquor twice as strong and half as dear;
Work if ye will, and, if ye will, be idle;
Who shall presume the people's will to bridle?

Lawyers shall spill their ink and tear their vellum,
Forget the meaning of a six and eight;
Their craft belongs to 'status ante bellum,'
And now is obsolete and out of date;
Scribblers and quibblers, we no longer need 'em,
Let musty law give place to lusty freedom!

Forensic jargon shall no more be spoken;
Away with judge and jury, wigs and fees!
Indentures, contracts, leases shall be broken,
And mortgagors shall mate with mortgagees;
When each owns all, and every man's a brother,
Where is the sense in suing one another?

If some among you feel the need of knowledge,
Set down your wishes, order what you please.
Open shall stand the gates of every college,
And all who care for gauds shall get degrees;
There may be use in learning, though we doubt it,
So many of us do so well without it.

If parsons stay, their sermons must be brighter,
Expound our doctrines and be half as long;
We set no store by crozier or mitre,
So sell the bishop's palace for a song;
Avaunt! ye deans; avaunt! all out-of-daters,
Who strut about in shovel hats and gaiters!

In days gone by, we thought a nation's head
Looked all the better with a crown upon it,
But now, provided it is coloured red,
We pay our homage to a cap or bonnet;
So many kings have played the fool or rogue,
Crowns, orbs and sceptres vanish out of vogue.

As we have willed that crime and sin shall cease,
And everybody be as good as gold,
We waste no more a penny on police,
Sheep need no dogs that live within a fold.
Soldiers and sailors all shall be disbanded,
Since all the world with peace is sugar-candied.

So, to our joyous shouts, Utopia rises,
As Ilium rose to great Apollo's song;
Nearing the goal of all its enterprises,
The world in rapture rolls itself along.
The lamb casts loving glances at the lion,
And hawks and turtles mate in England's Zion.

FREE WILL

WHAT is it strives within, when we have striven,
Or to ourselves have seemed to strive?
Are we as winds and waters blindly driven?
And who are they that drive?

Are they but random forces that, combining,
Keep for a term their balanced poise and stress,
Locked into shapes, whose intermittent shining
Men call their consciousness?

Forces that weave their web and then unravel,
Quiver as light, or vibrate into sound,
And, after years of unavailing travail,
Repeat the unmeaning round?

Is all that gives to life its grace and glory—
The mind that soars, the will that cries 'Be free'—
But evanescence, flashings transitory,
Of phosphor-'lumined sea?

'Not so,' there are who say, 'the powers that ever
Live in our life and work within the soul,
Move at the bidding of one vast endeavour,
Parts of an ordered whole.

That man is free who, from his elevation,
Knows that through him that purpose has been willed,
That, but for him in his appointed station,
Some part were unfulfilled.'

Is this then all? Man's glory is still withholden,
Is this the vaunted freedom of the will?
Though every link that binds him may be golden,
Man is in fetters still.

Not from without alone, but from within him,
Constraint may come, his soul in bondage be;
Till man can spurn the grace that seeks to win him,
He knows not liberty.

BY CONISTON LAKE

No fault it is of thine,
  If what I drew from thee I draw no more,
As brightly as of old thy waters shine,
  As sweet their music rolls along the shore.

'We take but what we gave,'
  (The poet sings[1]) the grace of opening flowers,
Glory of sunset, sparkle of the wave,
  In us alone they live, their life is ours.

If age bring clouded sense,
  If sin or sorrow strike the spirit blind,
A shrinking Nature shares our impotence,
  Till the lost beauty wakes in others' mind.

O folly of the wise!
  That measures all that is by all that seems,
Truth, beauty, goodness live, whatever dies;
  Though waning powers may catch but broken gleams.

[1] Coleridge.

TO THE SKYLARK

SWEET bird! whose song sets all our bards a singing,
   I, in my modest unobtrusive way,
Would follow, fresh fantastic praises bringing,
   If they had left me anything to say,
But when I think of something to thy credit,
I ever find some better bard has said it!

And so I silent sit and watch thee rising,
   Hoping the inevitable hour has come,
When, cloyed and sated with apostrophising,
   'Tis joy to thee to find a votary dumb;
Love may be theirs who lack the gift to show it,
As some sing out of tune, who never know it.

A CONSTELLATION

THE very type they seem—those clustering spheres—
   Of bright communion, radiant brotherhood,
That lives by interchange of hopes and fears
   And common effort bent on common good.
Each star turns on his fellow a smiling face,
All in linked splendour move with equal pace.

Yet, were love theirs, and could some luminous ray
   Shoot as a loving glance from friend to friend,
A hundred years might see it on its way
   Through the vast void, ere its swift flight should end;
And hearts and souls, that seem to mingle here,
As far apart may move as sphere from sphere.

TO A PARROT

O TELL in unambiguous phrase
   The meaning of that troubled glance;
Art thou perturbed by man's capricious ways
   And baffling circumstance?

Has some faint flickering memory stirred
   A momentary wish to be
Once more the gaudy predatory bird,
   That squawked in liberty?

If black embittered thought be thine
   Of some untold unburied grief,
Accept this proffered sympathy of mine,
   And give that thought relief.

A world of wisdom seems to sit
   Behind that bold embattled beak,
Invoke its aid, infuse some dash of wit,
   And speak, good parrot! speak.

Then full and clear the answer came,
   I gave one shuddering glance and fled;
Wake not the blushes of ingenuous shame
   By asking what she said!

AN IMPRECATION

I would some dread Serbonian Bog,
   Or dead Sargossa Sea,
Might swallow those who play the hog,
   On the road that is dear to me,
On the road where I trusted to amble and jog
   Till the days of senility.

Dust and disdain around they cast,
   With a glance that seems to say
' 'Tis ours to ride on the withering blast,
   And yours to go coughing away,
To cough like the gassed in the horrible past
   When the devil was having his day.

An age of force is born again,
   And we of its anarchs are,
The trampling hordes of Tamburlane
   And the Huns of Attila;
Then, on with her, run her amok and amain,
   Ye gods of the clanking car!'

SECOND YOUTH

If second childhood comes with age,
   A second youth should now be mine—
A youth whose fires have spent their rage,
   Which sips content its watered wine.

Though many a door to me be barred,
   Still stand the gates of wisdom wide,
And they that heavenly treasure guard
   May grant me glimpses long denied.

Though dust that clings to labouring years
    May choke the channelled paths of sense,
Bedimming eyes and dulling ears,
    Each age has its own recompense.

Much may be found, though more be lost,
    We know not what the haze may hide;
Then welcome, ere a night of frost,
    The slanting rays of even-tide!

'BEATI SUNT QUI AMBULANT

HARD is their lot, in these embittered days,
Who stand or walk upon the ancient ways!
When grudging years more strenuous feats denied
I bowed to fate and tramped the country-side.
Unclouded peace I found upon the road,
And health and pleasure followed as I strode.
With every breath I drew untainted air,
And, seeking beauty, found it everywhere.

But now, where'er I walk—as walk I must,
I turn, like shattered empires, into dust;
As the proud cars that bear the conquerors pass,
Each sense is shrivelled like the desert grass;
The tortured eye complains to afflicted ear,
One scarce can see, the other hardly hear,
And stifled thought, all loftier themes forgot,
Ponders perforce on our unequal lot.
Of dust and deity men compacted are,
The dust is mine, the god is in the car!

ECCLESIASTICUS

WITH shafts as keen, and with as sure a stroke,
   Wisdom her message sent through Sirach's son
And his dis-canoned book, as when she spoke
   Through the belauded lips of Solomon.

Here homely precepts, fit for an infant age,
   Join with rebuke that charged with thunder rolls,
Shrewd warning, kindly wit, illumes each page,
   Nor lacks there balm for stricken contrite souls.

'Bow down thine ear to them that know distress,
   Let thy feet wear the doorstep of the wise,
Sow not the furrows of unrighteousness,
   Hold back thy bread from him that truth denies.

'Seek thou the Lord and in His fear abide,
   Shun not reproof, from fretful cares be free,
Good is it when men's hearts and souls are tried
   In the fierce furnace of adversity.

'Faint hands and fearful hearts alike despise,
   In strength and meekness all thy tasks pursue,
On needless matters bend not curious eyes,
   Make straight thy paths, be to thy purpose true.

'Turn from thy sins, resolved to sin no more,
   Put from thee sloth, let hate and vengeance die,
The whisperer scorn'—So runs the old-world lore—
   'O House of Israel! seek the Lord Most High.'

THE RAINBOW

WHEN shall the rainbow arch be built,
That shall token be to the sons of men
That the Powers of Heaven have pardoned guilt,
And the world shall never be whelmed again?
     Soon, O soon may that rainbow rise
     From a blood-drenched earth to the pitying skies!

Of what shall that rainbow arch be made?
Of hopes that stood through the straining years,
By faith's unfaltering stanchion stayed,
With solder of sorrow and studs of tears;
     Legions of angels shall there be sent,
     To stretch that bow o'er the firmament.

What are the colours that there shall glow,
When the great bow bends to the angel's song?
Red shall be there, that the world may know
Its ruin was wrought by a flaming wrong;
     But the red shall fade and the sapphire's blue
     Proclaim that the Heavens their grace renew.

Purple and gold shall be seen subdued,
For on pomp and pride shall a seal be set,
They have worked for the world's disquietude,
And peace shall be visioned by violet,
     For the violet speaks of a soul that sighs
     For the love that pardons and purifies.

The green of Spring and the yellow and brown
Of Autumn meet in that rainbow's ray,
And the splendour of Summer shall sober down
To the tender tints of a dying day;
     And their blended sheen shall a symbol be
     That the hope of the future is harmony.

A STREET SINGER

WHO cometh here, that sings so heavily,
The astonied stones cry out in dear despite,
Lest that their weightiness outweighted be
By leaden drone? What brought thee to this plight,
And set thee here, discomfortable wight,
That on the bleak air pourest bleaker song?
If pence thou seekest, get thee from my sight,
And let this penny go with thee along.
Soothly men say, in wealth much virtue lives,
It blesseth him that goes and him that gives.

WINTER WISHES

WERE I deputed—to my vast content,
To order this disordered world below,
So charged with empire o'er each element
That seas would cease to rave and winds to blow
At my reproof, first would I bid the snow
(Whose falling ever robs me of my rest)
To arctic wastes and desolation go,
Or but adorn the loftiest mountain crest;
Earth in Spring's brightest drapery should be dressed,
Fell Winter blunt his sting, abate his spite,
Or be no more, and, as beseemed me best,
The rain should fall—but ever in the night,
Rude winds be tamed and blow but from the West;
Nature would then be kind and man be blest.

NAME AND NATURE

Who has not known (and felt vicarious shame)
Fair scene befouled by harsh ignoble name?
From such offence our Fens and Fells are free,
There name and nature meet accordantly.
Some names light-footed as a fairy dance,
Some statelier move with smooth soft assonance.
No crowded consonants clash an angry note,
No gutturals grate, or gurgle in the throat.
A name is thine, as gently lulls the ear
As thy low lapping wavelets, Windermere!
And some have deemed thy neighbouring waters shone
Fairer for their fair name of Coniston.
Lone Ennerdale and Ulva's winding lake
Please for their name as for their beauty's sake.
Their bordering peaks bear titles echoing far,
As full of sound as their own cataracts are—
Helvellyn, Glaramara, Helm and Scar,
While Duddon, Eamont, Eden, Leven, Kent
Fill more than anglers' ears with rich content.
Brathay and Rotha, Lowther and Lodore
Of pebbled raving speak and swelling roar,
While soft as ripples of an ebbing tide
Sound Aira, Elleray and Ambleside.
Nor lacks there music, fitness of sense and sound,
In homelier names in fen-girt Anglia found.
More charged with pastoral peace what names could be
Than Swavesey, Hemingford and Madingley?
Earith, where Ouse deserts his ancient bed,
Recalls wide watery wastes hill-islanded.
Like Esk and Greta, Granta, Ouse and Rhee
Tell their own tale, and tell it tunefully.

Quaintly bemoaning dearth or wild excess,
Wet-Sleddale matches Westley-Waterless.
Far-scattered hamlets, flanked by marsh and fen,
Bear names like Childerley and Eversden,
While, by the banks of classic creeping Cam,
Come Milton, Horningsey and Haddenham,
And clear as flute or storm-cock's opening note,
Sound Linton, Cantalupe and Caldecote.
Each village name its worth or story tells
In syllables as sweet as village bells.
O joy! that to these favoured regions came
Men skilled to mingle music with a name.

NOW AND THEN

ONCE the Father's word was law,
His to order and forbid;
Sons received with reverent awe,
All he said and all he did.
    Now he tells the startled skies,
    Things are ordered otherwise.

Once the Mother aped the queen,
Kept her court and reigned secure,
Round her, as she sat serene,
Daughters sat depressed, demure.
    Now her sky has lost its blue,
    She dare not think what daughters do.

Once the Husband thought the Wife,
Studying every wish and whim,
Ought to dedicate her life
To the task of pleasing him;
	Now that she has got the vote
	He sings upon a lower note.

Once the Master thought the men
Lived but to obey commands;
Sheep they were within a pen,
He was head and they were hands;
	His to fix their hours and pay,
	Now it isn't so, they say.

Once the Kings imagined they
Kept a helpless world from wrong;
Now, though crowns are cast away,
It somehow seems to roll along.
	Subjects say, and sovereigns too,
	Despotism doesn't do.

Parents, Husbands, Masters, Kings,
My advice to you is this—
Try to make the best of things,
None can fight with Nemesis.
	Murmur not at other's winnings,
	Each of you has had his innings.

THE THAMES

Since that dark hour of Britain's shame
When victor legions thronged thy shore,
O Thames! what memories haunt thy name,
What scenes that live for ever more!
    Scarce Tiber's self or storied Rhine
    Can boast a statelier past than thine.

Proud monarchs, Saxon, Norman, Dane,
O'er thee on blazoned prows have swept,
By thee in England's hallowed fane
The noblest of her sons have slept,
    And still around their honoured grave
    Sounds the soft lapping of thy wave.

Along thy paths of wandering foam,
With silver cross uplifted high,
Came he who, charged with power of Rome,
Purged England of her heresy;
    Alas! he did but wake again
    The fires that made appeasement vain.

Twice o'er thee to thy towered marge
A queen has sighed her way to death;
Thy billows rocked the gilded barge
Of haughty-souled Elizabeth,
    When, breathing words of high disdain,
    She fired the hearts that humbled Spain.

Twice hast thou seen—in Plague and Fire—
Thy waters thronged by flying fear;
From ashes of her funeral pyre
Thou saw'st the undaunted city rear
    Palace and spire and lordly hall
    Ringed round the rising dome of Paul.

On thy broad breast, mid wild acclaims,
The prelate-laden bark was borne,
That sealed the fate of bigot James,
And on thy flood he fled forlorn,
      When England shook from sea to sea
      With blasts of wakening liberty.

Full many a bright or shadowed scene
Uprises, as thy waves we view;
Still be to us what thou hast been,
Old Thames! that art for ever new;
      A nation's past, its weal and woe,
      Are mirrored on thine ebb and flow.

FEAR, SLOTH AND PRIDE

FEAR, oft-recurring fear,
  Has given the stag his nose and nimble pace,
And dowered the rabbit with the length of ear,
  That crowns his foolish face.

Sloth, undiluted sloth,
  Shrinking from effort, feeding like a blight
On honest toil, has atrophied the growth
  Of Turk and parasite.

Pride, over-weening pride—
  Mad lust of empire over all below—
Has made the cultured 'Hun' a homicide,
  And wrought his overthrow.

Life, ever-changeful life,
  For man and beast alike is but a school
Where some their lesson learn in strain and strife,
  While others play the fool.

THE ELM AND THE ICE-BERG

You may look with delight on my towering height
   And my broad boughs foliaged far,
But which of ye knows or can measure aright
The half of me grows in the gloom of a night
   That never has known a star?

Far foraging round may my roots be found—
   Let the doubter dig and see—
When his spade or his share touch my being's bound,
It will witness bear that a rood of ground
   Is alive and a-tangle with me.

The glittering berg, the mariner's foe,
   Rears pinnacled peak on high,
But few are there know how far below
That isle of emerald ice and snow
   Its dark foundations lie.

The berg and the tree may a symbol be
   Of the two-fold life of man;
In a sunless soil or a soundless sea
One part must live everlastingly,
   The other the heavens may scan.

A LAMENT

I WOULD I were as when I lay,
Dead comrades round me lying,
Scarce had I more of life than they,
But hope was mine that bitter day,
Now hope itself is dying.
 I would brave once more the thirst and pain
 To feel that hope in my heart again.

It whispered me of duty done,
Of strife and sorrow ended,
Of home and peace and of honour won,
Till, out of the glare of that ghastly sun,
The peace of heaven descended,
 And voices came from o'er the sea
 And hands outstretched to welcome me.

My foot is on my native shore,
But hope from my heart is shaken,
My dream of a home and of rest is o'er,
The bride that was mine is mine no more,
And my post has another taken;
 Ah happier had they let me die
 Where my lost comrades lay and lie.

AN IRON AGE

THERE are cottage homes in Devon
   That a little while ago
Looked like burnished bits of jewelled heaven
   Dropped by angel hands on earth below.

Forest-lovers out of Arden
   Might have lodged as blithely there,
There, forgetting their forbidden garden,
   Might have lived and loved earth's primal pair.

Each with flowery croft surrounded
   Glowed like Saturn in his ring,
Now o'er all the knell of doom has sounded,
   And we who sang their praises cease to sing.

Sheeted iron (corrugated)
   Glares on lichened roofs today,
Blotting beauty that with use had mated,
   Sweeping swallowed eaves and thatch away.

Devon! scarce the sight were sorrier,
   Hadst thou helm or aureole
Torn from hallowed head of saint or warrior,
   And, mocking, crowned it with a tinker's bowl!

'I CANNOT COMMEND A FUGITIVE
AND CLOISTERED VIRTUE'
(MILTON)

SMALL risk they run of doing wrong
    Whom no bold quest beguiles,
Who never hear the Siren's song,
    Or skirt Circean isles.

Ungirt, unproved, they saunter on,
    Or hug their souls at home,
Not theirs to ford life's Rubicon,
    And storm their way to Rome.

For them no lightnings glare without,
    No passions surge within,
By stiff conventions hedged about,
    They have no room to sin.

No wave from life's torn ocean breaks
    In their sequestered bay,
No trumpet-call their soul awakes,
    To challenge frowning day.

Sinless and smooth the path they tread,
    But dark and dire their doom,
Who, living, simulate the dead,
    And haunt their manhood's tomb.

When man's last dread account is given,
    And earth has passed away,
Full many a sinner mounts to heaven
    On swifter wing than they.

TURENNE

'ART thou trembling, body of mine?'
Said Turenne—the brave Turenne,
When, all along the embattled line,
He saw the lifted banners shine,
And his soul drank, like burning wine,
The acclaim of death-defying men,
 As loud his trumpets sang advance
 To the lilied hosts of France.

'Thou shalt tremble more' he said,
'Ere the set of sun,
Thou shalt pass through scenes of dread,
To the foremost fight be led,
Share their glory with the dead,
Or look on victory won;
 Bodies are but slaves of men'
 Said Turenne—the brave Turenne.

'Thou hast that aflame within thee
Scorns thy weakness, flouts thy fear,
And through tormenting flames should win thee,
Were all black Satan's horrors here,
 With every fiend that haunts his den'
 Said Turenne—the brave Turenne.

'Flesh may flinch, but spirit never,
Shrink and shudder, if thou wilt,
Onward shall it urge thee ever,
Till the last links of life dissever,
And thy latest blood be spilt;
 There shall be no trembling then'
 Said Turenne—the brave Turenne.

SOME APHORISMS

Who knows hate—knows nothing;
Who knows love—knows all;
They are but blind, that scorn their kind,
With love their scales shall fall.

Who keeps hope—keeps heaven;
Who has it not's in hell;
For hell is here, for all that fear,
With hope in heaven we dwell.

Who seeks wealth—seeks trouble;
They only treasure own,
Who barter cares for heavenly wares,
And live for love alone.

Who feels pride's in prison;
That man alone is free,
Whate'er his place, who knows the grace
Of true humility.

Who feeds strife shall perish,
In blank confusion fall,
Glory and fame shall turn to shame,
When love is all in all.

THRUST AND PARRY

LIFE'S seeming rise is but a subtler blending,
  A swifter pulsing of the powers that ran
In Earth's dim dawn, uncaused and never ending
  They move as wind, or masque as mind of man.
    No fountain higher than its source can rise,
    Life first and last is force, in ever-shifting guise.

Peace! Lives there nought, when some sweet strain is
      sounding,
  But wave-beat eddying air supremely stirred?
Earth's forces are not life, but life's surrounding,
  They are the nest that shelters, not the bird;
    Weave them but wisely, new-born grace is given,
    And forms earth-fashioned fill with molten ore from
      Heaven.

DUNWICH

(The last church-tower of Dunwich was destroyed by
the sea in November, 1919.)

LAST of a score of towers
  To fling defiant music o'er the sea,
That lion-like roared round and now devours,
  Thy vigil ends, Dunwich has ceased to be!

E'en while she crowned her state
  With mitred pomp in her meridian day,
The foe had rolled his thunders to her gate
  And hurled afar the challenge of his spray.

And now we mourn the fall
　From lone sea-bluff of her last lingering shrine;
It fell, as on Byzantium's ruined wall
　Fell, midst the Paynim, Rome's last Constantine.

Beyond that ruthless main,
　Still, swollen or shrunk, her old-time rivals stand,
But they that Dunwich seek shall seek in vain,
　They find but moaning sea and shifting sand.

THE 'SONS OF CONSOLATION'

DAYS that are empty may be filled with meaning,
　And evening make amends for wasted morn,
From careless reaping comes abundant gleaning,
　Life mid discarded ashes may be born.

Channels long choked, with weedy growth encumbered,
　May gleam in rippled glory once again,
Awakening music that has idly slumbered,
　And spreading verdure through life's parching plain.

Fret not, nor deem thine effort unavailing,
　Mark how, at shadowed eve, the birds will sing,
Though one by one the founts of hope are failing,
　Life owns more fruitful seasons than its spring.

The Sons of Consolation gather round me,
　And thus their wisdom platitudinous pour,
I sigh to think they leave me where they found me,
　But who was ever bettered by a bore?

LOVE'S RECOMPENSE

Ask not reward from Power above,
True heart! Disdain that prayer;
The heart's best recompense for love,
Is just love's presence there.

Ask only that a fitter place
For love that heart may be,
And that the heavenly guest may grace
That shrine eternally.

The stream that from the mountain flows,
Returns not on its track;
It scatters blessings as it goes,
But asks no blessing back.

It may not see those heights again,
Or take as it has given,
'Till, lost and mingled with the main,
It mounts in mists to heaven.

So is it with immortal love,
Unbartered, gushing free,
It gives itself till, drawn above,
It joins heaven's ecstasy.

'BACK TO NATURE'

(THREE INTERPRETATIONS)

'BACK to Nature! Let her lead you,'
Cried the Stoic long ago,
'She on Reason's food shall feed you,
Brace you with her ice and snow,
Like an o'ergrown garden weed you,
Till none but flowers of wisdom grow;
Trample passion, stifle feeling,
Thus the sick soul finds its healing,
And bears erect life's weight of woe.'

'Back to Nature!' cries Rousseau,
'Break from all the bonds that bind you,
Keep all the fires of life aglow,
Stiff conventions fling behind you,
Let the wild blood freely flow;
Launch your bark upon an ocean,
Where every wave is an emotion
And passion's tide swings to and fro.'

Cries Nietzsche, 'Back to Nature go!'
Power is life's ennobling feature,
Pity, man's insidious foe.
Lord it o'er your fellow creature,
What of ruth does Nature know?
Love and meekness are but weakness,
Steel the heart and strike the blow!

(*Chorus*) 'Back to Nature go.'

RED CLOVER

WHAT power has spread that film of red
O'er yonder field so fair?
' 'Twas I,' the farmer proudly said,
' I sowed red clover there.'
    Indignant buzzed the humble bee—
    ' You sowed, but owed the rest to me.'

Afar they fare, and drive the share,
Where sun and soil are kind,
They sowed their fields with clover there,
But left the bee behind;
    No flower with ruddy crest will glow,
    Then buzzed the bee—'I told you so!'

PEDAGOGY

STREW thick the path of studious youth
  With many a jagged stone;
Each stumble on the way to truth
  Will make it more his own.

Put fear in his rebellious breast
  Of what may hap behind,
The work that springs from interest
  Debilitates the mind.

Then ply the rod and play the Turk,
    Count milder measures vain,
Teach youth the truth that worthiest work
    Is work against the grain.

So learnt they, in our fathers' days,
    The little that they knew,
Some are there praise these strenuous ways,
    But they—thank Heaven—are few.

ALTERNATIVES

In days of Dionysian art,
And Saturnalian jigs and joys,
When players overplay their part,
And music masquerades as noise,
        What shall the staid Victorian do?
        Must he become ecstatic too?

Shall he affect a rapturous air,
Put wistful wonder in his eye,
Do something valorous with his hair,
And witch creation with his tie,
        Like Sirion skip and Hermon hop?
        Or be as pard and Ethiop?

Shall he denounce his former day,
And try to think new worlds are found?
Or, standing like a stag at bay,
Die with his antler in the hound?
        Or, Timon-like, in sullen rage,
        Seek out some moss-grown hermitage?

PEACE AND THE KAISER

(September, 1918)

Not as returning day,
Not as the first flower piercing its wintry clod,
Comes Peace to thee, but as that warning ray
Which wrote in fire 'Thy realm is rent away'—
The accusing finger of an angered God.

'Tis no soft wakening breath,
Bringing cool respite to thy fevered brow,
But the distempered air that followeth
The beating of the wearied wing of Death,
Which moans among thy shrivelling laurels now.

Thy boast has ever been
No power but Heaven's o'ertopped thy towering height;
Earth was for thee an ever-shifting scene,
Where thou—its moving centre—robed in light,
Resplendent shone, the embodiment of might,
Unequalled, unapproachable, serene!

Thy trust was in the sword,
Its ceaseless shaking and the World's dismay
Charmed thy gross nature, as some glittering gaud
Enthrals the savage, while a wolfish horde
Snarled round thee, hungering for their promised prey.

Thine was the felon's stroke—
The minèd sea, the smooth insidious lie,
The tiger-spring, at which a world awoke
And shook thy power on ocean, earth and sky,
Till imaged victory melted from thine eye,
And prostrate peoples crept from 'neath thy yoke.

Thy land lies desolate;
Thy people know thee now as we have known;
Their plaudits turn to mutterings of hate;
The tarnished trappings of thy former state
Hang limp and loose around thy tottering throne.

Had but thy spirit kept
Some touch of greatness, some redeeming trace
Of ruth or honour, vengeance might have slept;
Among the mourners some perchance had wept
To see the shadows deepening on thy face.

But who shall weep the fall
Of him who, swollen with insatiate pride,
Bade his rude legions trample over all,
Who made the imperial purple Freedom's pall,
And, so his glory lived, recked not who died?

MERTON HALL, CAMBRIDGE

AGE have we known that, by some gift of grace,
   Could blunt the point of Time's pursuing spear,
Guide his despoiling finger, and bid it trace
New lines of beauty where it would deface,
   And paint a smile where it had planned a tear.

Such age is yours, O venerable walls!
   Unconquered yet, that harbour mine and me;
Soft as the tread of one whom pity calls
To succour pain, on you Time's footstep falls,
   And century whispers century 'Let them be'—

Ye hold your place where once the Mercian met
   The Anglian bounds, when Rome had passed away;
Ye had your rising when in sorrow set
The star of England's first Plantagenet,
   Who snatched his realm from rude baronial sway.

A century passed, and, in like troublous days,
   The favoured home of him ye came to be,
Who, to his glory and eternal praise,
A beacon reared, neath whose soul-wakening rays,
   Glowed Oxford like a sunset-'lumined sea.

Walter of Merton, prince in Church and State,
   But princelier, nobler, that he loudly blew,
In tones that to our times reverberate,
The trumpet-call bade England educate
   Her strenuous sons, would she her health renew.

Two centuries more, and here as owner came,
   Charged with like zeal, the twice discrownèd king,
Who wore the red rose till it drooped in shame,
And stored its fragrance in a hallowed name,
   In cloistered courts and chantries lingering.

Long may ye stand and speak to altered times,
   Old walls! of scenes and glories passed away,
Fenced by your aged yews, bee-murmurous limes,
And towering elms, while Great St Mary's chimes
   Float round and lull you in your soft decay.

'THE BIG FOUR'

Four pillars of a trembling Earth!
  Four watchers of a boding sky!
To you a new world clamours for its birth,
  Ye watch an old world die.

No power that erring man has known
  Can match your world-encircling sway,
No fiercer light shone ever on a throne
  Than streams on you today.

Your words fall charged with weight of doom,
  Your frown can darken all our years;
Your smile can pierce an anguished empire's gloom,
  Dry a crushed people's tears.

If yours should prove a faltering hand,
  And swerve at passion's fitful call,
Once more a tortured world in arms shall stand
  And hope from Heaven shall fall.

As Earth's new order ye create,
  Draw from the old its warning clear,
Bring to your task a heart too high for hate,
  Too resolute for fear.

ALSACE-LORRAINE

'Tis but in part Cassandra sees,
When through her boding vision sweep
Dim-phantomed—Priam on his knees
By Hector dead, wild eyes that weep,
The captive maid, the funeral pyre,
And towered Ilium's shroud of fire.

Her vision had not strength to rise,
Above that crowded grief and see,
Where, far beyond those reddened skies,
Troy rose again in Italy,
Saw not Aeneas cleave the foam,
To found the Achaeans' conqueror—Rome.

More keen those weeping eyes that saw
Enslaved Alsace and lost Lorraine,
When, crushed beneath an alien law,
They dragged an ever-galling chain;
Through every tear there shot a ray
Of distant recompensing day.

O loved and lost and found again!
That day is here! What hosts are these,
That throng thy streets, Alsace-Lorraine?
What strain comes floating down the breeze?
What banner heralds their advance?
'Tis France is here, and ye are France!

AMERICA 'GOING DRY'

(An appeal to Bacchus)

GREAT son of Semele! Has it come to this?
   What shall thy hunted harassed votaries do?
Must they renounce the wine-cup's gladdening kiss,
Let cranks and bigots bar the gates of bliss,
   Shake from their heaven its blue?
From such sad sobering let thy thyrsus screen us,
Rise with thy nymphs, thy satyrs and Silenus!

Cancel this folly! Over-rule this law!
   Bid its rash authors ponder Pentheus' fate,
Recall the frenzied scene Cithaeron saw,
Let thy dread presence freeze their souls with awe,
   Their cankered zeal abate!
Proclaim to all who from thy cult would wean us,
'Twill last as long as faith in Mars and Venus.

DISILLUSIONMENT

MY hope soared high, like the amorous band
   That mounts with the mating bee,
Then it sank as an elephant sinks in the sand,
   Or as sediment sinks in the sea.

The world, I had hoped, of its strife was sick,
   And had turned to a better way,
Since a simple sum of arithmetic
   Had proved that it does not pay.

141

I had hoped that hate would be out of date
    In the order about to be,
But alas! it is rash to anticipate,
    And wiser to wait and see.

For vain is the vision of love as lord,
    Alas for his golden reign!
Hate wearied as we of his work abroad
    And has followed us home again.

PEACE IN PERIL

EXPECTANT earth shone all a-bloom,
And music broke from every tree,
When Orpheus, from the nether gloom,
Led back his lost Euridice.
        Alas! at very gates of day,
        One backward glance—she sank away.

She too shall sink—long captive Peace,
Whom we, with wild rejoicings hail,
If, bidding cares and trouble cease,
We let the backward look prevail,
        And urge once more the soulless life,
        That fed the springs of hate and strife.

Ah! What avails it that we rose
Indignant from the soft caress
Of ease, drank deep of death and woes,
And half redeemed life's sordidness,
        If Peace we see—the longed-for bride—
        Drawn back upon an ebbing tide.

EPILOGUE

A CANDID kindly much-enduring friend
Has read these verses through from end to end.
Each piece he pondered with a puckered brow,
As though he wished to praise, but knew not how.
At every gibe or jest he paused awhile,
The stifled yawn transfiguring to a smile.
At last he sighed and said, 'One thing you lack,
Abundant bread is here, but where's the sack?
From first to last, though wide the ground you cover,
One piece alone on love and ne'er a lover!
Save where a beetle, to his ghoulish bride,
Droned out a drivelling dirge before he died.
Verse without love is life forlorn of breath,
Gasping for air and dallying with death.
Take up, for pity's sake, the abandoned pen,
Infuse some dash of Love's wild oxygen.'

True, true! my friend, yet silence your upbraiding,
What would Love say to senile serenading?
The golden harps of youth may sport with fire,
Our fumbling fingers twang a leaden lyre.
Yet all find heaven, whose vehicle is verse,
In flaming chariot some, some in the homelier hearse.